FRENCH PILOT

Volume Three
Raz de Sein to Belle Ile

MALCOLM ROBSON

Nautical Books
Macmillan London

ISBN 0 333 32925 2

First published in Great Britain 1983 by
NAUTICAL BOOKS
an imprint of Macmillan London Ltd
4 Little Essex Street
London WC2R 3LF

Associated companies throughout the world

Caution
While great care has been taken in the compilation
of this book, neither the author nor the publisher
can accept responsibility for any inaccuracies and
omissions or mishaps arising from the work.

Photoset by Rowland Phototypesetting Ltd
Bury St Edmunds, Suffolk
Printed in Hong Kong

Contents

Introduction

Facing the prevailing SW winds, Biscay, land of fierce seas and strange legend, smiles under a reputation many nautical miles from the truth. Seen those sheltered rivers? Been up those sandy estuaries? Ever tried those busy little fishing ports? Sailing from the Channel, once round the corner of Ouessant and through the Raz, suddenly all is different . . . the weather pattern changes, the sun is hotter, seas are bluer.

This guide is for the chap who wishes to wander along the coast, among the islands, up the rivers; leisurely cruising. It is not for the owner who uses his boat merely for transport, or goes out for a day's sail to return to his home harbour at nightfall. Nor is it for those more modern sailormen whose seafaring is chained to the soullessness of a marina. So why not buy a few French charts, fit a pair of legs to your boat and get a close-up of those entrancing places you have been seeing only through binoculars? Within a week or so you will be speaking French and—if merely in self-defence—enjoying garlic. 'Every civilised man', reminds Ben Franklin, 'has two homelands. And one of them is France.'

The French treat electric supply as a jest, and sewage not at all, but when it comes to marking their coasts I know of no other country to equal theirs. The lights are numerous, the buoys enormous, the beacons prolific and anything with enough space carries its name in big letters. First class maintenance of the entire system is the year-round job of the *Ponts et Chaussées baliseurs* whose skippers incidentally are mines of information.

There has been a dramatic change in the atmosphere along the French coast toward *plaisanciers*, the direct result of the atomic proportions of the boating explosion. The marinas are filled as fast as they can be built and as a result they are wastelands of parked vessels often unused, seldom provide places for visitors and are somewhat expensive. Fishing harbours which formerly welcomed, or at least tolerated, visiting boats now sternly segregate amateurs from professionals. There remain all those small ports, many drying, some difficult to enter, but all uniformly glad to see the occasional visiting yacht.

You won't find this a treatise on navigation; locating your position before looking for pilot marks is elementary coastal plotting. Also, since inflation is as sure as sunrise, costs haven't been mentioned. Nor does this pretend to be a restaurant guide: what was top last year may be a *discothèque* this. But if there is one thing I would most humbly beg you to accept advice about, it is . . . legs. Every fishing boat, every yacht, motor boat, from 1 to 100 tons fits *les béquilles*. Fewer than one in ten of the harbours I describe doesn't dry, so without legs and a straight keel for taking the bottom you might just as well save the cost of this book. Since they were built before divers, few older harbour walls project further than LAT, so you will just have to get used to berthing single-legged, either against a quay or another boat. In any port, naturally, working fishing boats come first, so you will often have to dry in mid-harbour using both legs. You will therefore need a ladder: either folding, made from rope, or rigid. My own home-made one is typical of thousands: it fits to a leg when dried out in the open; it hangs from a ladderless (therefore often vacant) part of a high quay; it is used for bathing; it is a gangplank.

Notice how sparing I am about amenities. Whether the banks open on Friday or Saturday seems of less importance than knowing there will be 4·1 metres in an hour alongside the quay.

Lobster pots need particular care since they have floats on long buoyant rope, to cope with the tidal range. Often their owners lay them in narrow, rocky channels and with scant heed to traffic. And from traffic so to transport. After years of cruising with collapsible bikes we now have folding mopeds. With either you will see something of rural France apart from quaysides, thus making those remote anchorages even more pleasant. What's worse than a two-mile heavily laden walk in the opposite direction to a café?

Customs now oblige pleasure boats to use fuel taxed at the same rate as road users, and as quayside pumps only provide low-duty fuel to fishermen, this can become a problem. If you can take enough you might persuade a small road tanker to deliver by hose, otherwise take your cans to the filling station. Fuel Oil *domestique* is forbidden for yachts.

Unless you use the tiny but ubiquitous International Camping Gaz cylinders, bottled gas is another perennial headache. Nobody will exchange British containers and I know of no handy plant where they can be filled, so the best solution is to carry enough spare gas on board. Paraffin users will laugh coarsely at all this fuss—until they too have to gather a few sticks for cooking—their tipple is called *pétrole* and may be bought with increasing bother at paint shops.

The information has been arranged from the north-west, Raz de Sein to Belle Ile, and for convenience the area is chopped into three parts, see Fig. 2. There is no overlap either in charts or in marks.

French and Breton words in the text, unless they are names, are printed in italics, with a translation in the Glossary if required.

Finally, while information has been checked, sorted and rechecked, still errors can creep in so neither the publisher nor I can be responsible for mistakes or omissions. But, please, if you find any faults or you can supply additions, could you write to me in Sark?

Charts

Any mention of charts in this book refers to my sketch charts. The three areas G–I are in Fig. 2: detailed charts are indexed in Figs. 3, 4, 5. Charts are metric and soundings, drying heights and elevations have been reduced to LAT. Liberties have been taken to envelop collective dangers and there are only three basic contours: HAT, LAT and the 3-metre line. Anything below this can't be of great interest to yachts. In the text a figure in italics and underlined (e.g. *1·2m*) shows the height in metres drying out above chart datum (LAT). One

Fig. 1. Key to chart symbols

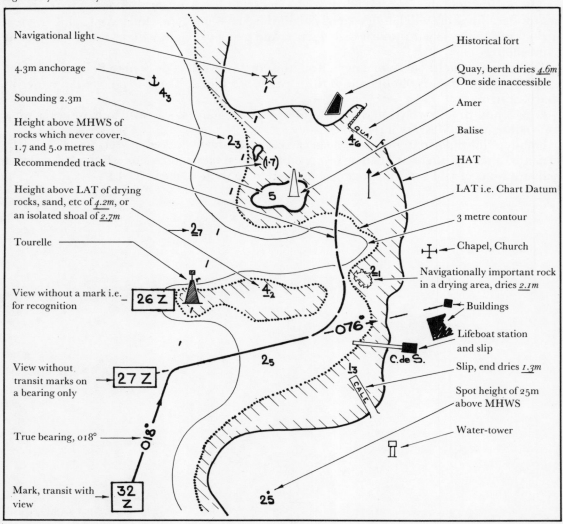

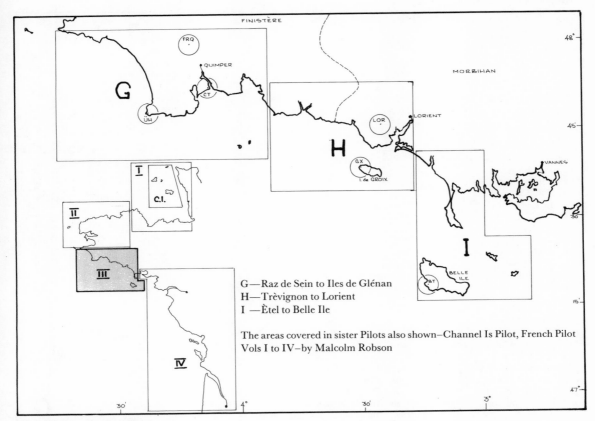

G—Raz de Sein to Iles de Glénan
H—Trèvignon to Lorient
I —Ètel to Belle Ile

The areas covered in sister Pilots also shown–Channel Is Pilot, French Pilot Vols I to IV–by Malcolm Robson

Fig. 2. Index to book sections

big difference between French and British charts is in the height of rocks which never cover, but I've followed the Admiralty by showing heights as measured above MHWS. On modern French charts these heights are measured from 'mean level' or about half tide, although on older ones they are shown as the height above chart datum, very confusing. Headway under bridges is the same and I give this as above MHWS. Bearings are true; those of lights from seaward; of transits as seen in the view. Symbols are generally those on Admiralty Chart 5011, alas without colours, Fig. 1. Section that down the middle and you have approximately Fig. 12. I very seldom show rocks—the area is wall-to-wall anyway—unless of significance. Their elevations I've guessed sometimes to point the difference between 20m and 5m; who cares if they really should be 17·8 and 5·3? Drying ground may contain rocks, sand, shingle, mud, or a mixture of the lot. Similarly the quality of the bottom is ignored; however no anchorages are shown in known poor holding.

Compass roses are absent, the side margins are true north. East margins show minutes of latitude and tenths, i.e. nautical miles and cables. The south gives minutes and tenths of longitude. Where these are omitted I draw a scale. A cable = 185 metres = 608 feet. To give some clue to the terrain, spot heights are sometimes shown in metres above MHWS.

Stupid mistakes are inevitable in constantly changing from British to French charts; swapping from metres to feet; confusing abbreviations like B = black = *blanc*. Therefore my

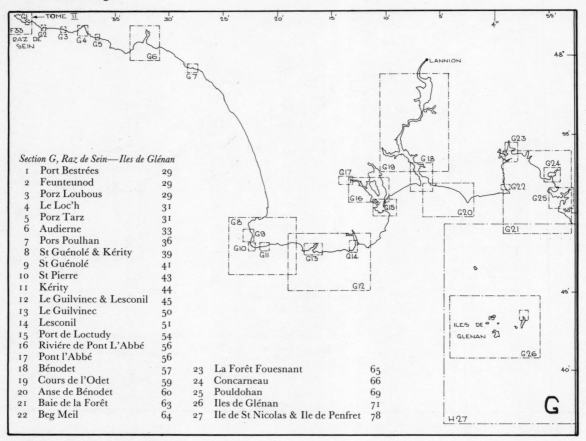

Fig. 3. Index G. Raz de Sein to Ile de Glenans

Within the figure:

views and charts, abbreviations, colours, lights are all in French. My charts are never intended to substitute for proper navigational charts. But when you buy these, buy French because Admiralty coverage is meagre and the scales are small. Some 9 charts cover the same area as 22 French ones, which can be bought from most Admiralty agents in the U.K. and in many French ports. Keep them corrected from Notices to Mariners, clean, dry and flat for they cost double; Admiralty charts are indexed in Fig. 6, French small-scale passage charts in Fig. 7. Larger-scale detail French charts are shown in Fig. 8.

A single word, light, describes lighthouses, light beacons, light structures; characteristics, which often change, are never given, only height above MHWS; sectors are occasionally referred to. In thick weather or gathering dusk it is comforting to recognise quickly a beacon light, which is why I have included so many of their profiles. A *balise* is a pole with a topmark, but if it's on a rock it might have a concrete base for strength. A *tourelle* is of masonry or concrete, commonly like a capsized flowerpot and always with a topmark. A disused *tourelle* is painted white. It is promoted to a *phare* (lighthouse) if it is given a light, indicated by a star. *Amers*, many of which are relics of an era before lights and uniform buoyage, are daymarks, more often white than coloured and very often form one of a pair of transit marks. They never

8

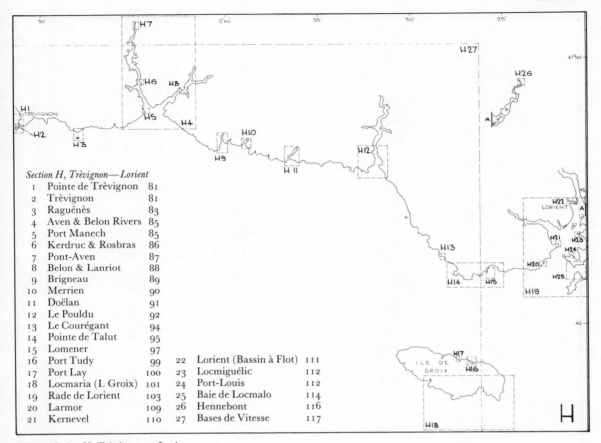

Fig. 4. Index H. Trèvignon to Lorient

carry navigational topmarks, are mostly in stone or concrete, and look like slim pyramids or cylinders. Walls on land are *mur-amers*, very rare. Hang a light on an *amer* and it becomes a *phare*. Publications of the *Service Hydrographique et Océanographique de la Marine* (SHOM) with Admiralty equivalents are:

Catalogue-Index A, Europe et Méditerranée	4A	Catalogue of Charts	NP 131
Atlas des Courants de marée, de Brest à St Jean de Luz	552	Tidal Stream Atlas, France West coast	NP 265
Radiosigneaux (1ᵉʳ volume)	91	List of Radio signals	ALRS(2)
Annuaire des marées, Tome I, France	5	Tide Tables Vol 1, Europe	NP 200
Feux et Signeaux de Brume, Manche et Océan Atlantique est	C	List of Lights, Vol D, Eastern Atlantic	NP 77
Symboles et abréviations figurant sur les cartes marines françaises	1D	Symbols and abbreviations	5011
Instructions Nautiques, France nord et ouest	C2	Biscay Pilot	22

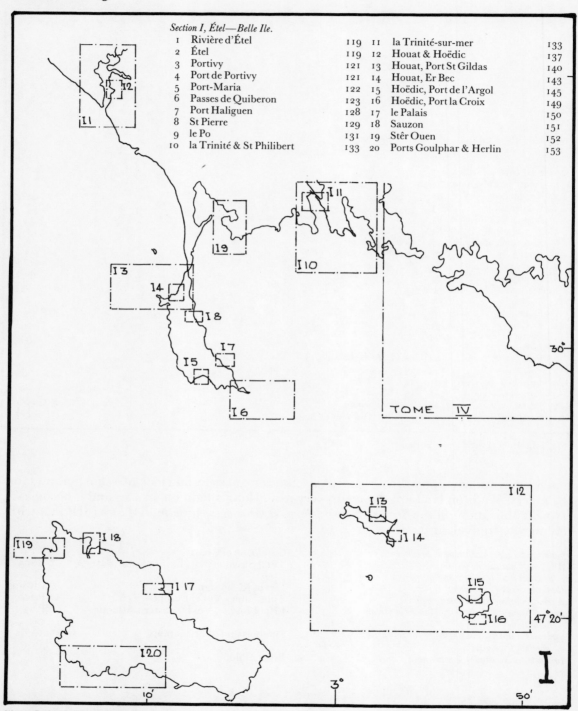

Fig. 5. Index I. Etel to Belle Ile

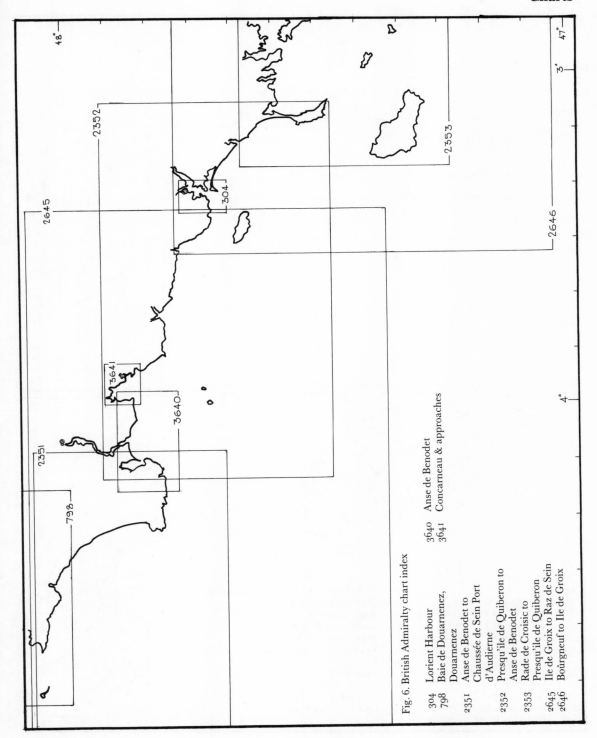

Fig. 6. British Admiralty chart index

304	Lorient Harbour
798	Baie de Douarnenez, Douarnenez
2351	Anse de Benodet to Chaussée de Sein Port d'Audierne
2352	Presqu'île de Quiberon to Anse de Benodet
2353	Rade de Croisic to Presqu'île de Quiberon
2645	Ile de Groix to Raz de Sein
2646	Bourgneuf to Ile de Groix
3640	Anse de Benodet
3641	Concarneau & approaches

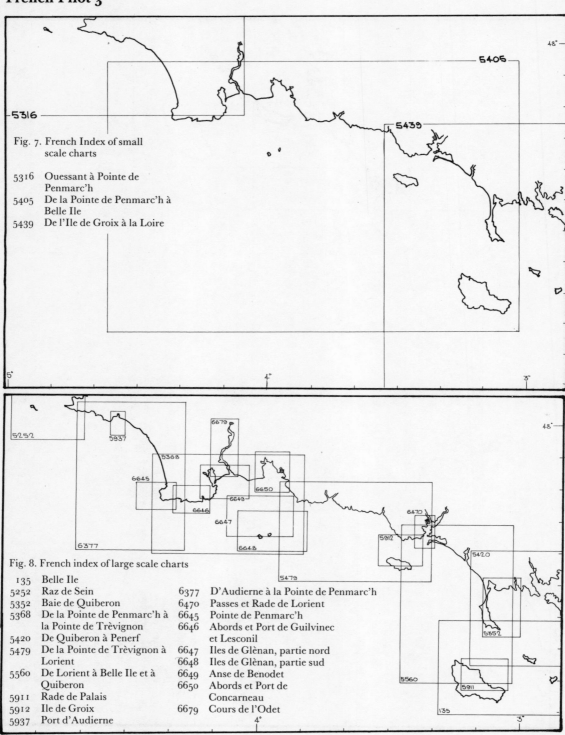

Fig. 7. French Index of small
scale charts

5316   Ouessant à Pointe de
        Penmarc'h
5405   De la Pointe de Penmarc'h à
        Belle Ile
5439   De l'Ile de Groix à la Loire

Fig. 8. French index of large scale charts

135	Belle Ile
5252	Raz de Sein
5352	Baie de Quiberon
5368	De la Pointe de Penmarc'h à la Pointe de Trèvignon
5420	De Quiberon à Penerf
5479	De la Pointe de Trèvignon à Lorient
5560	De Lorient à Belle Ile et à Quiberon
5911	Rade de Palais
5912	Ile de Groix
5937	Port d'Audierne

6377	D'Audierne à la Pointe de Penmarc'h
6470	Passes et Rade de Lorient
6645	Pointe de Penmarc'h
6646	Abords et Port de Guilvinec et Lesconil
6647	Iles de Glènan, partie nord
6648	Iles de Glènan, partie sud
6649	Anse de Benodet
6650	Abords et Port de Concarneau
6679	Cours de l'Odet

Radio Beacons

These are shown on Fig. 2 as a circle with the identification letters inside. All are continuous.

Name	Type	Ident.	Frequency kHz	Emission	Range miles	Position N	W
ECKMÜHL (1)	RC	ÜH	289.6	A2	50	47°47.9′	4°22.4′
PTE DE COMBRIT (1)	RC	CT	289.6	A2	30	47°51.9′	4°06.8′
PLONÉIS	Consol	FRQ	257.0	A1	—	48°01.1′	4°12.9′
ILE DE GROIX (1)	RC	GX	289.6	A2	50	47°38.8′	3°30.6′
LORIENT/LANN-BIHOUÉ	Aero RC	LOR	294.2	A1	80	47°45.7′	3°26.4′
BELLE ILE, GOULPHAR (2)	RC	BT	303.4	A2	100	47°18.6′	3°13.7′

Several of the above stations are grouped in the following sequences with the beacons listed, at one-minute intervals. Full details are in Admiralty List of Radio Signals—Vol 2 ALRS(2)

(1)		(2)	
Eckmühl	ÜH	Belle Ile	BT
St Nazaire	NZ	Ile de Sein	SN
Pte St Mathieu	SM	Pte de la Coubre	LK
Pte de Combrit	CT	Les Baleines	BN
Ile de Groix	GX		

Marks

Alignments, transits, lines, marks, they all mean one thing—a pair of objects one behind the other—which is all this book is about. Inshore pilotage depends entirely on marks, which word also describes a church, an *amer*, a house. A channel mark is when an alignment passes between dangers on both sides. A clearance mark keeps you away from dangers on one hand. A breast mark is secondary to a main mark, is roughly abeam, and usually tells when to turn, i.e. quit one mark and take another. How much to deviate from a mark, yet still be safe, can only be judged from charts giving enough detail. Occasionally I have stressed one side or the other. The distant mark is given in the text before the nearer one; the sign '✕' means 'by' to avoid confusion. A typical view is in Fig. 9—line 12Z a tower on a hill ✕ a beacon on a rock. Sometimes the marks are not in dead alignment as when the dotted rear mark is opened. In Fig. 9 it is opened to the SW but to avoid any mistake I would write 'a tower to the right of a beacon on a rock'. This is safest when required instantly to change from an ahead to an astern transit. When going along using a stern mark, it is pointless and dangerous to look

Fig. 9. Typical transit view

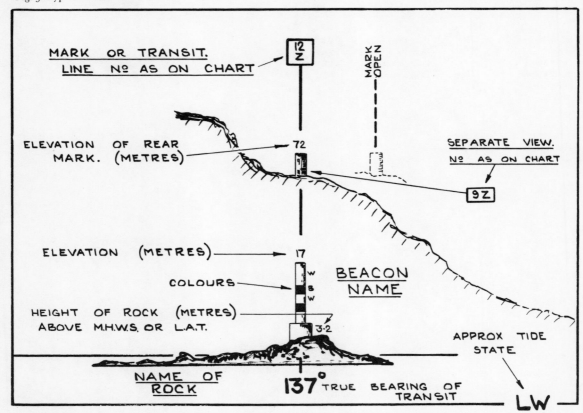

ahead only. Make a check for lobster pots, other boats, etc., then turn your head and concentrate on the transit. Have ye no faith in my marks?

All the marks have been sailed or motored over, according to tide, in our 44 foot sloop *Hephzibah*; she draws 2·10 metres and from her decks, her cockpit, her crosstrees I have made the sketches. May I therefore quickly agree with all you art critics? But I'm a sort of seaman and not an artist; try struggling with wet paper, one hand on the chart and another on a bearing compass, binoculars under your arm, half an eye on the sounder, bellowing into a tape recorder—all at once. Then repeat the whole lot because it's too late for the tide, again since there's too much swell, or it's neaps instead of springs, better scrub it for today anyway for it's too misty to see the marks!

Perspective has been fiddled and detail omitted, both for clarity. If an object is framed, this shows that it is out of position. If of use I have sometimes shown the approximate tide level, but only LW, HT and HW, on average tides (BM, MM, PM). Numbering of the lines is easy and I've tried to keep them in sequence. Charts are prefixed by the letters of their section (G1, G2, G3). Views in that section are suffixed by the same letter (25G, 26G, 27G). There are TWO kinds of transit numbers:

Within a SQUARE   —A view with a transit on a chart, of the same number.
Within a RECTANGLE—A view of something, drawn large for recognition. The view may have a
                              bearing.

A useful tip is to do your 'homework' well in advance of entering an unknown harbour. Draw, on your own chart, my transit lines, adding the mark number, page reference of its view together with its true bearing.

Safety

France looks after her citizens who take to the sea by a system of licences for boats and examinations for skippers. There are some 20 weather forecasts daily (more in summer) and a list of times, frequencies and automatic telephones is given in a free leaflet *La Meteo* from any *Douane, Bureau du Port* or *Inscription Maritime*. The leading shipping forecasts, though times are liable to change, are:

Le Conquet (1673, 1876, 2691 kHz)—0733, 1633, 2053 hours GMT in French.
St Nazaire (1722 kHz)—0703, 1703 GMT in French.
BBC (200 kHz)—0015, 0625, 1355, 1750 CLOCK times.

   The equivalent to coastguard stations are semaphores. These show storm warnings and are at prominent points:

> Pte du Raz
> Penmarc'h, St Guénolé
> Ile de Groix
> Port Louis
> Quiberon
> Belle Ile, le Talut
> Belle Ile, Pte de Taillefer

   The headquarters of the French lifeboat service for Biscay is C.R.O.S.S.—A, Château de la Garenne, 56410 Étel: Tel (97)52.35.35. Lifeboat stations, 24-hour watch, are at:

> Penmarc'h
> Le Guilvinec
> Loctudy
> Trévignon
> Ile de Groix
> Étel
> Belle Ile, Le Palais

Marks and Transit Lines

Tides

Unlike the areas covered in my three previous Pilot books (Normandy, Channel Is and Brittany) the Bay of Biscay has neither the large tidal range nor, in consequence, such fierce currents. So I have scrubbed tidal flow diagrams and instead give you in Fig. 10 the strength and direction of currents at selected points. Except at these places and at river mouths the tidal currents along the coast, within this volume, seldom exceed 1½ knots.

At any port in France you can pick up, free from any newsagents, a local tide table. This gives the day's times of high water (PM) and low water (BM). Alongside each is a figure, a 'coefficient' which is proportional to the range of tide, morning or evening, on that particular day.

Coefficients vary between 45 at neaps (*Morte eau*, ME) and 95 at springs (*Vive eau*, VE) though for equinoctial tides they can be as high as 120 and as low as 20. The table in Fig. 11 shows the heights of high and low water, springs and neaps, at several well-spaced places; you will see that there is little variation. Though there is a rather complicated way of calculating more exactly, it is really quite accurate enough to estimate for those days when the coefficient differs significantly from 45 or 95. Thus for a coefficient of, say, 70 (half way between 95 and 45) you could take a height half way between the springs and neaps figures.

Fig. 10. Tidal currents

Port of reference: Port Louis, Lorient

Hours	Between Penmarc'h & Iles de Glénan N47° 41′ W4° 12′			Chaussée de Teignouse N47° 27′ W3°04′		
	direction degrees	spring knots	neaps knots	direction degrees	spring knots	neaps knots
−6	349	0·6	0·3	315	1·0	0·5
−5	023	0·6	0·3	337	0·5	0·3
−4	070	0·6	0·3	020	1·8	0·9
−3	119	0·4	0·2	045	3·0	1·5
−2	140	0·3	0·2	—	—	—
−1	160	0·5	0·3	—	—	—
High water	190	0·7	0·4	090	0·5	0·3
+1	190	0·7	0·4	135	1·0	0·5
+2	200	0·5	0·3	180	1·5	0·7
+3	230	0·5	0·3	225	3·5	1·7
+4	260	0·6	0·3	—	—	—
+5	285	0·9	0·5	—	—	—
+6	310	0·9	0·5	—	—	—

Fig. 11. Tidal heights

	springs		neaps	
	MHWS	MLWS	MHWN	MLWN
Audierne	5·2	0·7	4·0	1·9
Kérity	4·8	0·6	3·7	1·7
Port Louis	5·0	0·6	3·9	1·7
Belle Ile	5·2	0·6	4·0	1·8

Tidal definitions are explained below and are graphically shown in Fig. 12.

HAT (Highest astronomical tide) = **PHM** (*Plus hautes mers*) and **LAT** (Lowest astronomical tide) = **PBM** (*Plus basses mers*) are the levels which can be predicted to occur under average meteorological conditions and under any combination of astronomical movements.

MHWS (Mean high water springs) = **PMVE** (*Pleine mer de vive eau*) and **MLWS** (Mean low water springs) = **BMVE** (*Basse mer de vive eau*) are the average rises throughout the year on two successive tides when the moon is at 23½° declination and the tide is greatest.

MHWN (Mean high water neaps) = **PMME** (*Pleine mer de morte eau*) and **MLWN** (Mean low water neaps) = **BMME** (*Basse mer de morte eau*) are for the same conditions as above but when the tide is least.

Just one reminder . . . BST, GMT or French time, but not a combination of all three. So when using tide tables remember that French time is one and sometimes two hours different from British.

Fig. 12. Tidal definitions

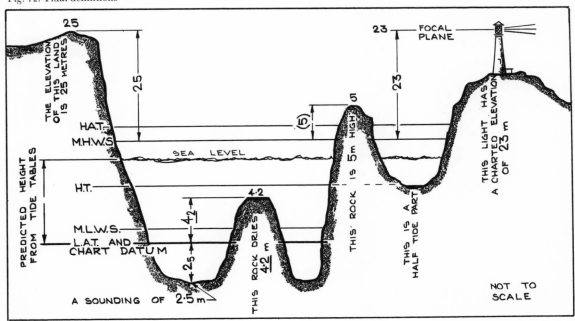

General Information

Customs. Pleasure boats arriving in France from abroad may only enter at a port with a *douane*, must have ships' papers, crew list and stores inventory, must fly international day or night signals. With whimsical Gallic logic Customs go on to say that by 'tacit declaration' and provided you arrive by sea, don't trade, run immigrants or charter to French citizens, you are free to come and go as you please. They can, and sometimes do, take a random check and can board your boat within 20 miles of the shore. The system is under threat of change.

Immigration. Passports only, required but seldom asked for, unless quitting the country by some other route. You will need them for cashing cheques and for *poste restante* mail.

Health. Certificates not required. If you need medical treatment in France see the Foreign Office leaflet 'Essential information for U.K. passport holders'.

Pets. Crippling fines if you bring a mammal back to the U.K. and practically a death penalty in the Channel Islands.

Money. Credit cards everywhere and all banks cash travellers cheques with no limit—or, with a Eurocard, cheques on U.K. banks. You mustn't take away more than 5000 Frs in notes.

Security. I've never locked my boat in any part of France and see no reason to start.

Duty Free. Can be bought wherever there is a willing chandler in a customs port.

Speed limits. 5 knots under motor within 300m of the shore.

Mopeds. Visitors, whose mopeds under 50 cc are licensed in their own EEC countries, may use them in France without further documentation as long as the riders wear crash helmets, keep off motorways and use cycle ways where available.

Buoyage

The promised change from the previous excellent French system to the new IALA buoyage is now complete in Biscay. This fresh look at maritime marking devised by the International Association of Maritime Authorities is that now used throughout Europe and the daytime marks are shown in Fig. 13.

Except for lighthouses and leading marks it is used for all fixed and floating marks. Objects are painted in four colours, lights have three. The five types are unambiguous:

LATERAL marks are on the sides of channels, the sense being that when coming in from seaward.

CARDINAL marks show where navigable water is in relation to, i.e. FROM a danger. Note that the French *ouest* (west) is abbreviated to the English W. CW means Cardinal West etc.

ISOLATED DANGER marks are built on or moored over a danger with navigable water all round.

SAFE WATER buoys are for mid-channels and landfalls.

SPECIAL marks are for military areas, traffic separation, outfalls, etc.

Whether you are looking at a *balise*, buoy, *tourelle* or pierhead, it is the topmark and, to a lesser extent, the colour which are the clues. That is why I have drawn, in Fig. 13, the dotted shapes, which vary considerably in practice. Abbreviations:

Blanc	b	White
Aux éclats	é	Flashing
Fixe	f	Fixed
Jaune	j	Yellow
Aux occultations	o	Occulting
Rouge	r	Red
Scintillant	sc	Quick flashing
Scintillant rapide	sr	Very quick flashing
Vert	v	Green

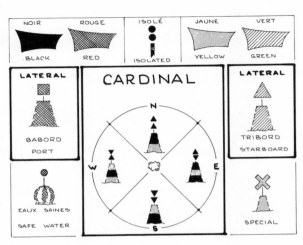

Glossary

Only words in the text and on charts are given. Breton words are in capitals. In this Celtic language letters are frequently interchanged, i.e. G–K–C'H, S–Z, G–W, B–V–P. An interesting dictionary of Breton– French is published by: Librairie de Finistère, 51 rue du Château, Brest 29N.

ABER	River mouth	Dog-leg, zig-zag	Two courses parallel, but offset, staggered
About	E.g. south-about is to set a course to leave an object to the north	*Dragué*	Dredged
Amer	Daymark	*DU*	Black
Ancien, -nne	Disused, old	*Duc d'Albe*	Mooring dolphin, pile
Anse	Small bay, cove		
AR, AN, AL	The	*Écluse*	Lock
AVEN	River	*EL, EN, ER*	In the
		ENES, ENEZ	Island
Balise	Perch, pole beacon	*Épi*	Spur of a quay
BANN, BENN	Height		
BAS, BAZ, BATZ	Shallow	*Feu*	Light
Basse	Low rock	*FEUNTEUN*	Fountain
Bec	Point	*Fosse*	Ditch, channel
BEG	Point	*FROUDE*	Rapids
Beniget, beniged	Gap		
BENVEN, BOSVEN	High rock, stack	*Gare SNCF*	Station, French railways
BIAN, BIHAN	Little	*GARO*	Red deer
Bili, vili	Shingle	Gateway	Course between two objects
Blanc, -che	White	*GLAS*	Green
Blanchi	White painted	*Goulet*	Narrow entrance
Bouchot à moules	Stakes for mussel culture	*Grève*	Sandy beach
Boue	Rock mostly submerged	*Gris, -e*	Grey
Bouée	Buoy	*GUEN, GUENN,*	
BRAS, BRAZ	Big	*GWEN*	White
Brise-lames	Breakwater	*Guérite*	Small watch tower
Cailloux	Gravel, stones	Handrail	Passing around an object, or several on the one hand
Cale	Slip		
C de G	Corps de Garde, watch house	*HIR*	Long
C de S	Canot de Sauvetage, lifeboat station	*Isolé*	Isolated
Chapelle, église	Chapel, church		
Château d'eau	Water tower	*KARREG, CARREC*	Rock
Cloche, Clocheton	Bell, turret	*KER*	House, hamlet
Clocher	Steeple, belfrey	*KREAC'H,*	
Crossroads	Where two or more marks meet	*CREAC'H*	Hillock
		KREIZ, CREIS	Middle
Damier	Chequered		
Demie	Half tide rock	*LANN*	Monastery
Déroché	Cleared of rocks	*LEAC'H*	Flat stone, place
Déversoir	Weir, spillway	*LEDAN*	Wide
Digue	Stone dyke	*LOC'H*	Pond, mere

MARC'H	Horse	*Raz*	Race
Marégraphe	Tide recorder	*Robinet*	Tap
MEAN, MEN	Stone, rock	*Roche, ROC'H*	Rock
MELEN	Yellow	*Rocher*	High rock
MENEZ	Hill	*Rouge, RUZ, Rousse*	Red, reddish
Menhir	Standing stone	*ROZ, ROS*	Wooded
MERC'H	Daughter, girl	*Ruisseau*	Rivulet, stream
Méridional, -e	Southern		
MEUR	Great	*Sal Br.*	Signal de brume, fog signal
MEZ	Seaward, wide	*Seuil*	Cill, sill
MOR, VOR	Sea, salt water	*Sifflet*	Whistle
Mouillage	Anchorage	*Son*	Blast
Moulin	Windmill, mill	*Sonde*	Sounding
Musoir	Pierhead	*STER*	River, creek
Neuf, -ve	New	*Terre plein*	Levelled area near quay
NEVEZ	New	*Tête*	Head
Nez	Nose	*Tirant d'air*	Headway, clearance
Noir, -e	Black	*Tirant d'eau*	Draught
Nouveau, -elle	New	*TOULL*	Cave, hole
		Tourelle	Navigational tower
Occidental, -e	Western	*TRAOU*	Low, west, valley
Oriental, -e	Eastern	*Traverse*	Intersecting channel
		TREAZ, TREZ	Sandy
PELL	Distant	*TREIZ*	Passage
PEN	Head, headland		
Phare	Lighthouse	*UHEL*	High
Pierre	Stone		
Pignon	Gable	*Vanne*	Sluice gate
Plat, -e, tte	Level, flat	*Vert*	Green
PLO, PLOU, PLU	Parish	*Vieux, Vieille*	Old
PORS, PORTZ, PORZ	Harbour, inlet	*VIR*	Needle
POUL, POULL	Roadstead, pool, lagoon		
Presqu'île	Peninsular		

Acknowledgements

There are two reasons why this book doesn't pretend to be a literary gem. For a start it's mostly pictures, isn't it? And though it has been a most pleasant exercise in communication, there is nothing in it which is original; other folks' advice, other people's ideas. Pilots have helped, commercial skippers have cautioned, yachtsmen have confessed secrets; here a lead, there a kindly chunk of advice. I can't think of an example when I was refused help. I've already drunk their health on board, but here is the place to shout *Yëa-a-mad* to all those who joined in the research ... Myrtle Green, Beth and Dennis Hurden, Captain Louis Lecoublet, John Lintell, Ann and John Moorshead, Bill Pethick, Freddie Torode, Commandante Richard Winter and my wife, Joan (who also co-researched much). Oh yes, and don't let us forget dear old *Hephzibah*, who looked after us all so well—she looks a shade tired after a non-stop flit in and out of some 180 harbours.

My sketch charts are based on French charts with the sanction of M. l'Ingénieur Général de l'Armement EYRIES, *Directeur du Service Hydrographique et Océanographique de la Marine*. I am truly grateful for his Department's help.

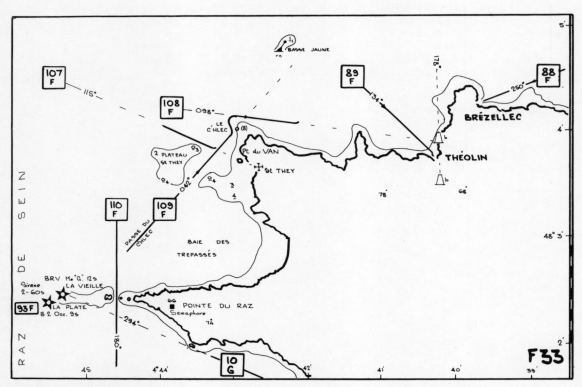

Chart F.33 Pointe du Raz

G   Raz de Sein to Iles de Glénan

The first 30 miles of rock pilotage spans part of what was the ancient kingdom of the Duchy of Brittany. Its capital is still Quimper, alas no longer accessible to masted boats. For us, having just been squirted through the Raz de Sein into Biscay proper, it is a smartish port turn along the high south coast of the Sizun peninsular. Between the Raz and Audierne there are five tiny, practical joke harbours. In most you can come alongside, albeit with some care and in fair weather. Facilities are nil, shops far away and if you are a sailor who cannot face up to life outside a marina, then you won't need your binoculars.

I have to take you back to chart F33 in my Volume II (Port Blanc to Ile de Sein). On it is shown

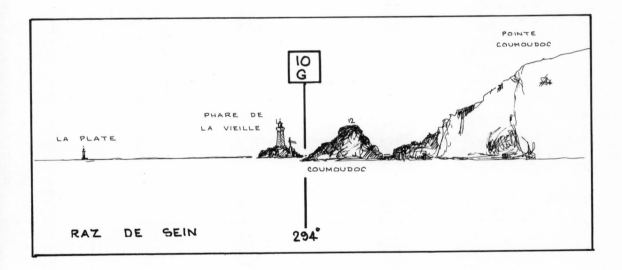

10G La Vieille lighthouse seen to the left of the only off-lying rock Coumoudoc, which is the danger mark to keep you clear of all coastal dangers. 3 cables east of Coumoudoc is our first joke.

PORT BESTRÉES

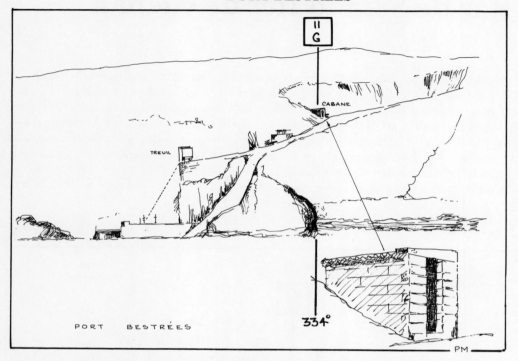

11G A concrete hut ✕ a bluff below the roadway. A few fishing boats moor here in summer but the west side of the *platforme* has a clean bottom for drying out, chart G1.

FEUNTEUNOD

Useable, but only just. Chart G2 shows the partly destroyed quay.

12G The left side of the only house in sight ✕ the root of the stone quay. Anchor among the half dozen boats off the slip.

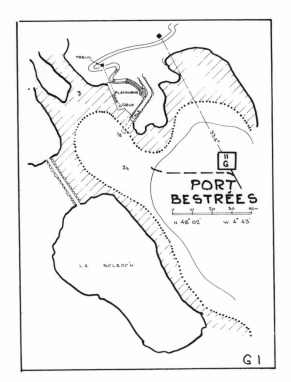

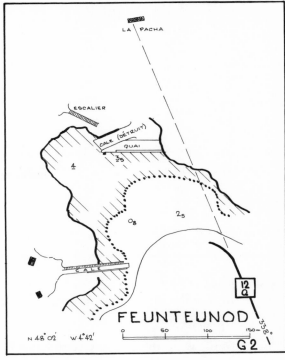

PORZ LOUBOUS

Chart G3 shows this rather gone-out-of-business harbour.

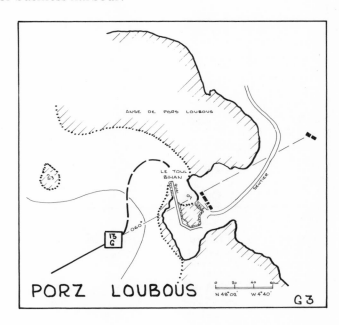

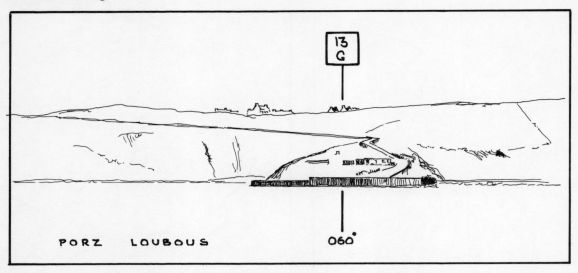

PORZ LOUBOUS   060°

13G A group of farm buildings ✕ the leftmost of a row of fishing huts. Moor four square to various rings to the east of the quay. Shops in Penneac'k 500m up the steep path.

LE LOC'H

This half-mile wide shallow bay is on chart G4 and to clear a drying rock Basse du Loc'h, take

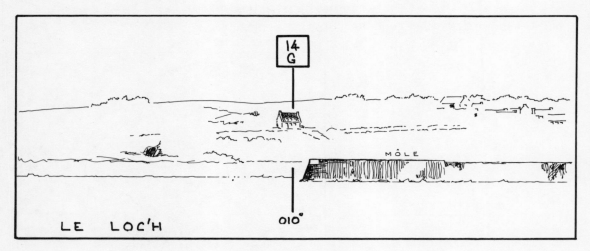

LE LOC'H   010°

14G an isolated white house ✕ the white patch on the end of the quay. The bottom is hard, clean sand and parts of the north side of the quay can be used for drying out.

PORZ TARZ

This is the last and smallest of these harbours, chart G5.

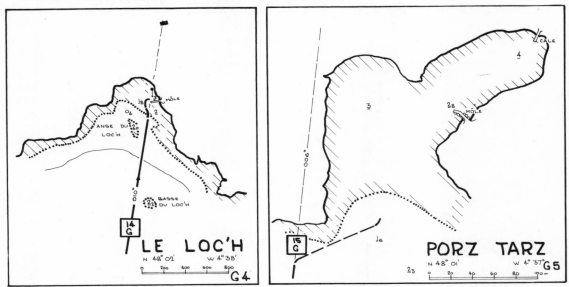

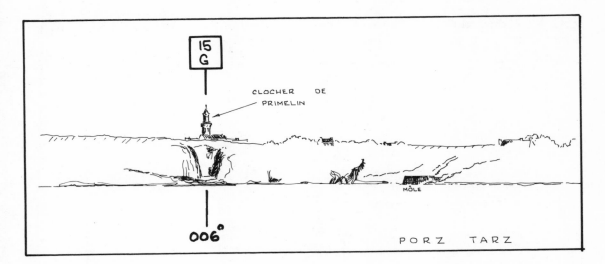

15G Primelin church ✕ a steep cove to the west of a beach. A useful dinghy landing is at the mole, though the NE part has level patches suitable for beaching. One km to the shop in Primelin.

AUDIERNE

Enough of those cracks in the rocks and on to chart G6, Audierne, a proper harbour and fishing port on the mouth of the river Goyen. Entrance is as easy by night as by day.

1—Main entrance

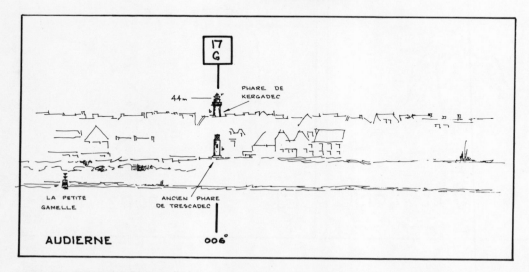

17G Kergadec light ✕ the disused light of Trescadec, almost on the beach. Kergadec is a sectored light, same bearing. When 3 cables before Ste Evette breakwater, take

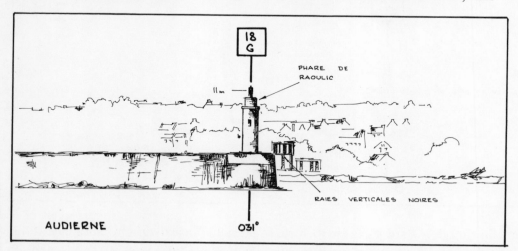

18G a vertical black and white building just to the left of Raoulic light, which takes you to the dredged channel.

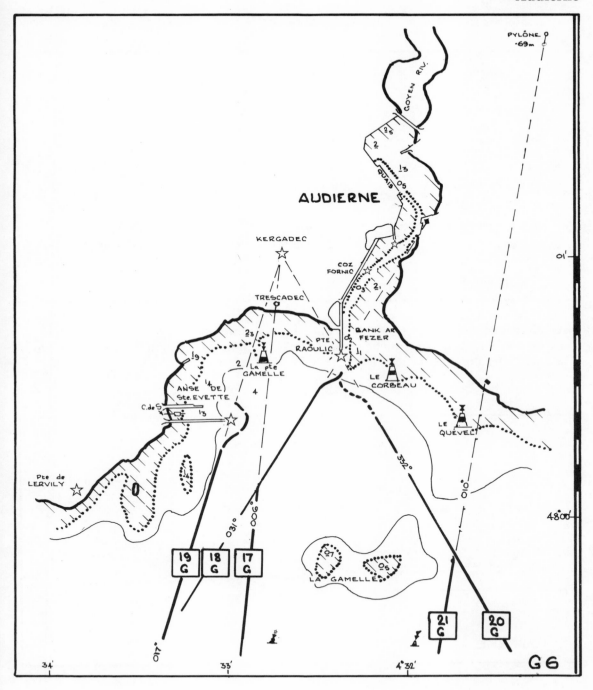

2—Ste Evette

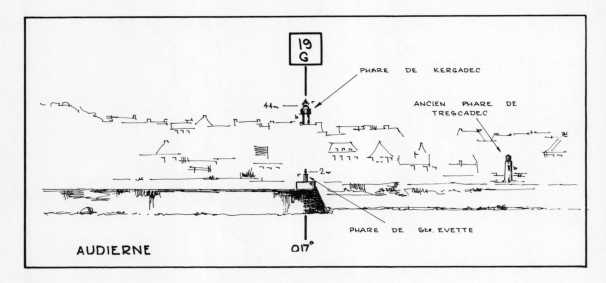

19G Kergadec and Ste Evette lights in line. Allow a cable off the breakwater—it is foul all along its northern face—and anchor or take one of the many buoys in the Anse de Ste Evette. The 250m long slip must be left clear for the Ile de Sein ferries.

3—SE entrance

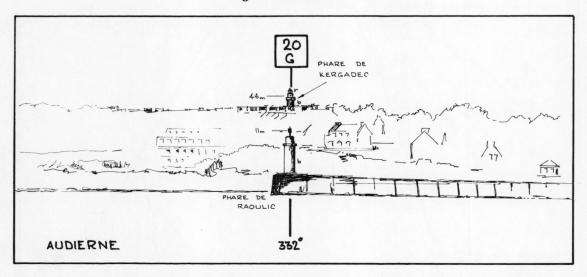

20G Day and night, the lights of Kergadec and Raoulic in line clear La Gamelle. If coming from the south take

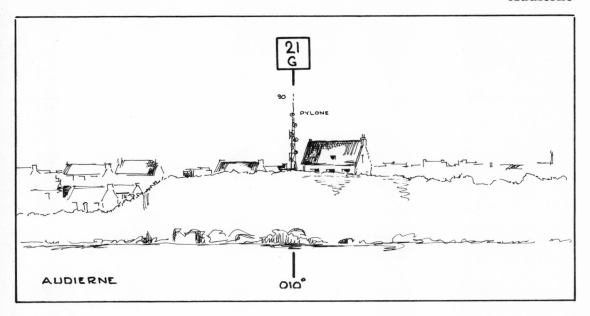

21G a telecommunications tower × an isolated white house right on the coast. Being a fishing harbour, *plaisanciers* are discouraged in the town itself. But try drying out near the bridge, close to the 2·5m sounding, out of everybody's way. The bar at the entrance needs respect; give this harbour a miss if there is a swell. Keep about 15–20m east of Raoulic light and maintain this parallel with the mole as far as Coz Fornic light, which carries its name. Audierne has everything for the commercial fishing fleet.

PORS-POULHAN

From Audierne southward lies 15 miles of west-facing shore before the shelter of the several harbours near Penmarc'h. But just over three miles away on chart G7, there is the drying harbour of Pors-Poulhan.

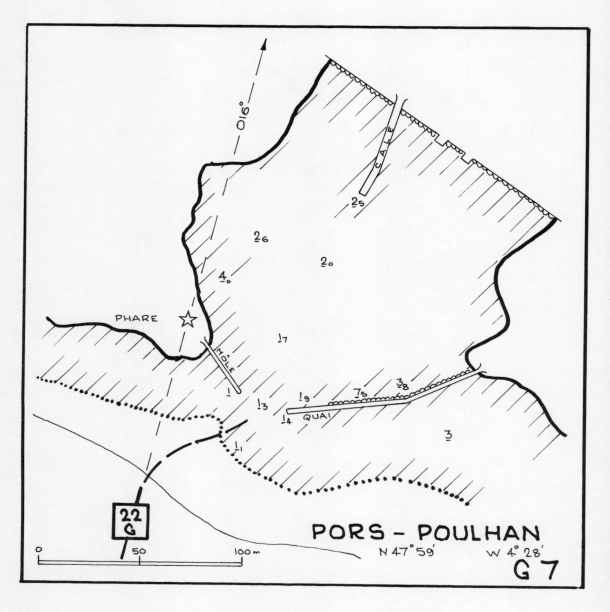

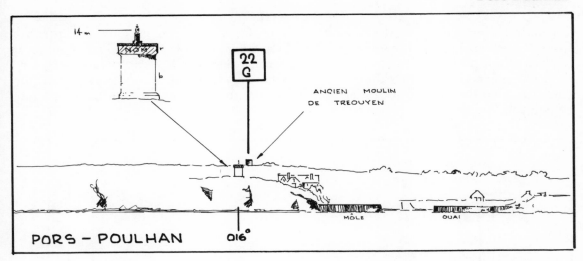

22G An old windmill × the main light. When midway between the pierheads don't turn too sharply to port, rocks lie under the east quay. There are mooring buoys in the central part of the harbour; a good place is near the _2·6m_ sounding on the west side.

St GUÉNOLÉ

Less barren, ringed by rocks, the Penmarc'h peninsular offers interesting pilotage. There are five safe harbours among the rocks, the first three are on chart G8. St Guénolé is a typical modern fishing port, home of fifty or so ocean-going trawlers together with all their necessary services, engineering, radio, ship repairs, etc. Chart G9 (p.41) shows the only practicable entrance, from the west. You can take these marks with confidence with or without a gale behind you, day or night.

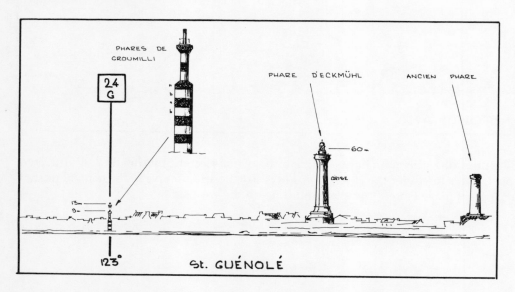

24G The two black and white lights of Groumilli, in line or very slightly opened to the left. There is 9·0m until the *petite passe* where it drops to 2·5m. When within a cable of Scoëdec, there is a breast mark for a port turn

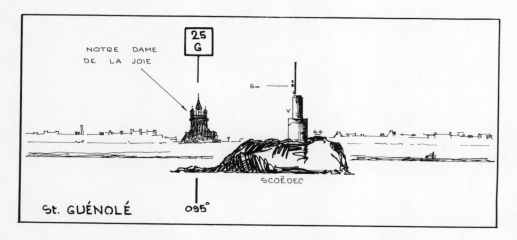

25G Notre Dame de la Joie just to the left of Scoëdec rock. From here pick the second transit

38

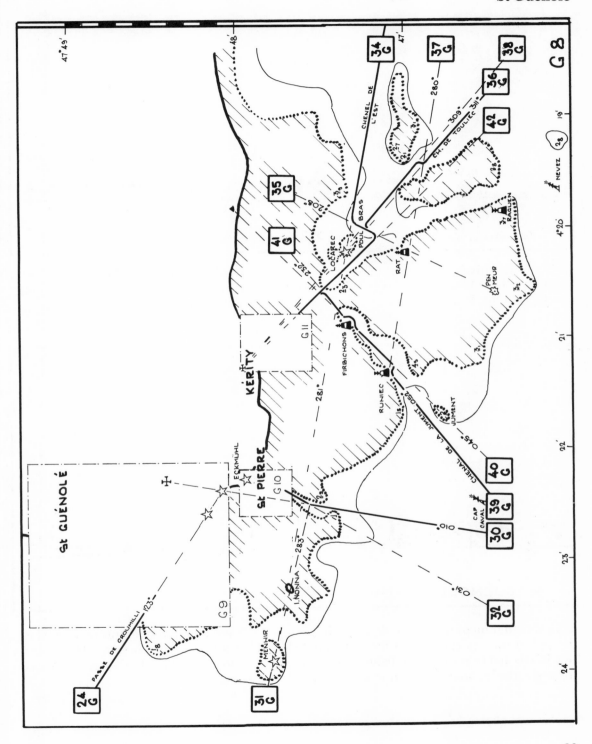

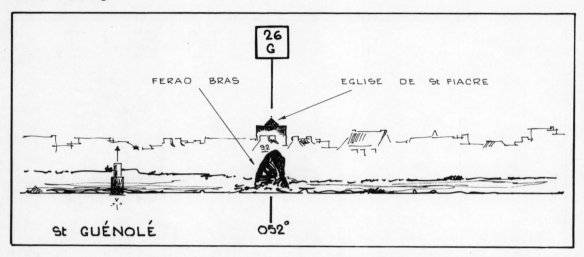

26G the stumpy square tower of St Fiacre ✕ an unmistakeable rock *9·2m* Ferao Bras. Now you will see the first of the channel buoys, but the final mark is a little difficult to pick out, except at night. It is

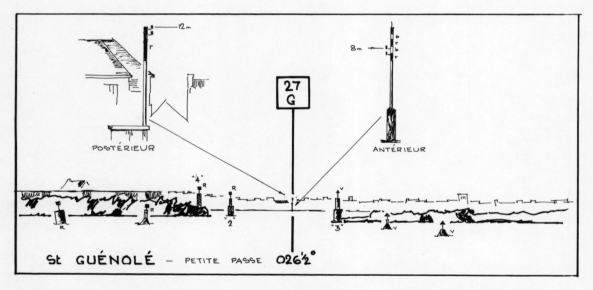

27G the alignment of the two lights of the *petite passe*. It is enough to steer midway between the 3 stb'd and 2 port *tourelles*. Once into the sheltered harbour, then where to go? All the west side is devoted to commercial fishing. Anchorage can be found, if the tide allows, on the east (opposite the lifeboat slip) or north of the slip shown as *2·0m*.

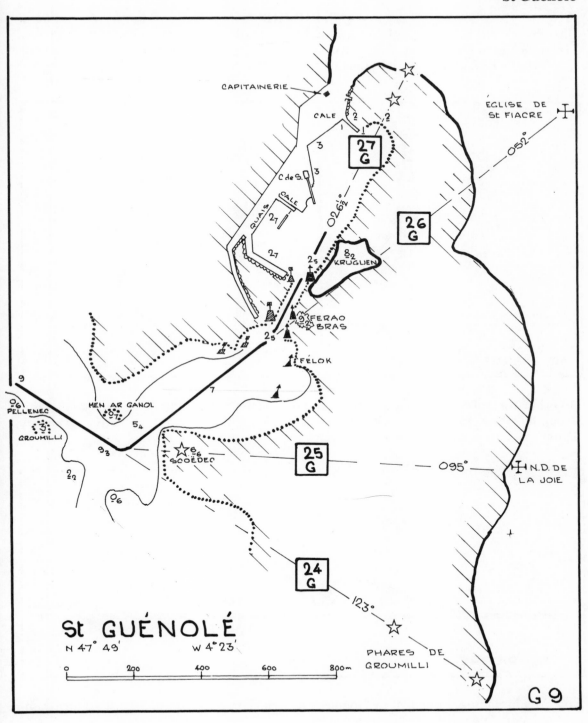

St GUÉNOLÉ
N 47° 49'   W 4° 23'

0 — 200 — 400 — 600 — 800m

G 9

St PIERRE

Directly below the massive lighthouse of Eckmühl nestles a tiny drying harbour, St Pierre. Like its neighbour to the east, Kérity, it dries too soon to be of use for fishermen. On chart G8 (p.39) a mile ESE of Menhir light the first mark is clearly defined.

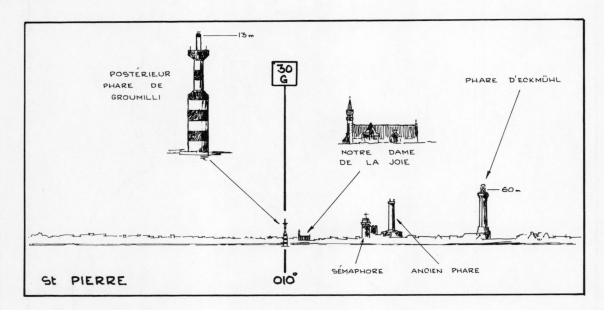

30G The spire of Notre Dame de la Joie, standing alone, to the right of the back light of the Groumilli black and white twins. About 4 cables off the grey granite of the Eckmühl lighthouse, look to the west for a breast mark

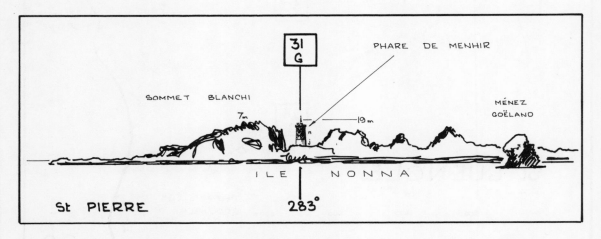

31G Menhir light × a notch in Ile Nonna 7·0m high. This is the cue for a 20° stb'd turn onto the final mark. You will now be on chart G10

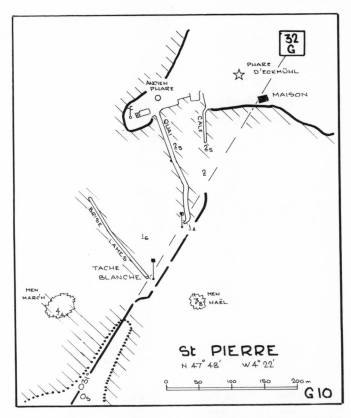

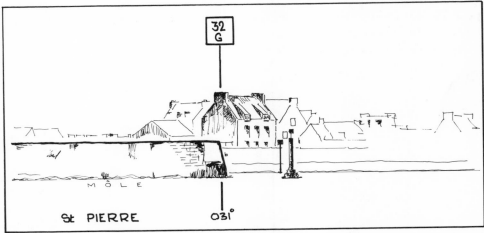

32G the chimney of a large house ✕ the white patch on the end of the SW breakwater. When 50m off the port *balise* come 25m to the east, leave the second *balise* also to port and there you are, in a room-sized snug harbour. The bottom dries about *2·5m* and is sand. Shops are a few metres distant and St Guénolé is only 2km away.

KÉRITY

Here is another drying harbour, large and seldom used and worth a serious study in contrast to the busy commercial traffic of nearby St Guénolé and Le Guilvinec. It has 3 channels, all on chart G8 (p.39). All three end on Poul Bras a cable off Locarec light. From there you can proceed into Kérity.

Here is the order:

1—Poul Bras from Chenal de l'Est
2—Poul Bras from Chenal de Touliec
3—Poul Bras from Chenal de la Jument
4—Kérity from Poul Bras anchorage

1—Poul Bras from Chenal de l'Est (2·6m)

This is the usual approach from Le Guilvinec and it starts about half a mile SW of the entrance, see chart G12 (p.48). The lead-in mark is

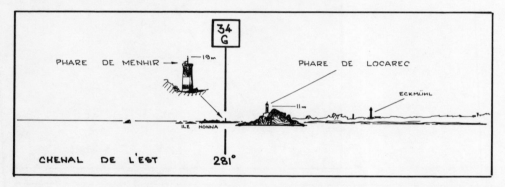

34G Menhir lighthouse to the left of Locarec rock as shown. When about 3 cables off the light, look for a port turn onto

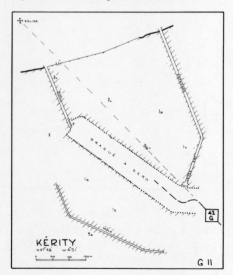

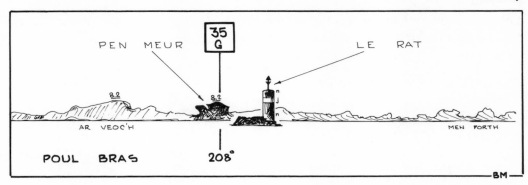

35G Pen Meur (like a Tortoise) to the left of Le Rat *tourelle* (CE). You are then· in the anchorage in 3·7m, sand.

2—Poul Bras from Chenal de Touliec (2·1m)

From either of the two entrances to Le Guilvinec, see chart G12 (p.48) the first mark is

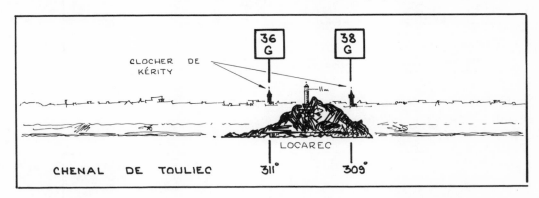

36G Kérity church to the left of Locarec light. For convenience two churches are shown in the same view, each a slightly different distance from the light. When ¾ cable from Locarec, there is a breast mark for a slight dog-leg.

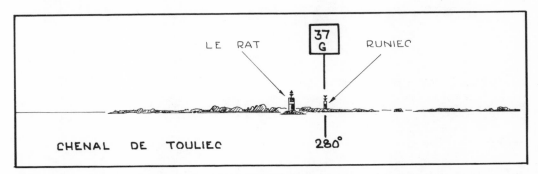

37G Runiec *tourelle* (CS) × Le Rat *tourelle* (CE). Then steer north for 100m until

38G Kérity church again, but this time to the right of Locarec. Carry on until you join view 35G (p.45) Pen Meur to the left of Le Rat *tourelle*.

3—Poul Bras from Chenal de la Jument (*0.3m*)
From near to the lit buoy Cap Caval (CW) the first marks are clear and man-made,

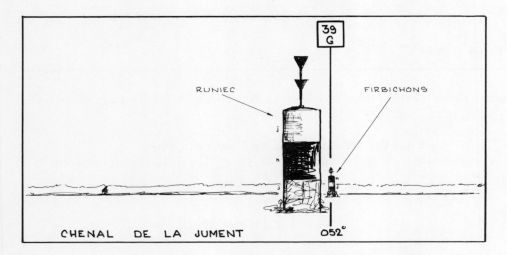

39G Firbichons *tourelle* (CE) × Runiec *tourelle* (CS). When 100m off Runiec, make a handrail east-about to find

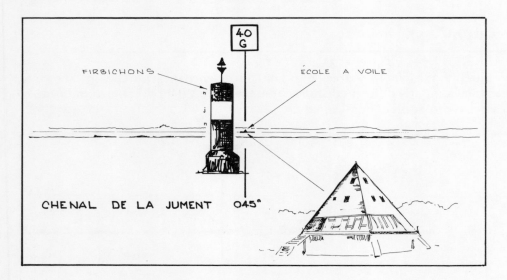

40G a pyramidal house on the distant dunes to the right of Firbichons *tourelle* (CE). Make another handrail, again to the east, round Firbichons and take a back mark,

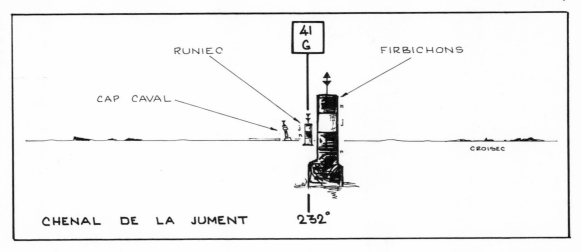

41G Runiec and Firbichons *tourelles* in line, either side, until the final mark for Kérity comes up.

4—Kérity from Poul Bras (*o·5m*)

The entrance mark is unambiguous and takes you onto the harbour chart G11 (p.44) from all the previous 3 channels, i.e. Poul Bras.

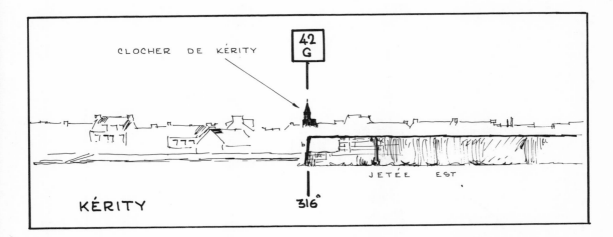

42G Kérity church × the white patch on the end of the east jetty. Once inside there is room for many boats on legs in the centre or against the quays. Shops are nearby and a frequent bus runs to St Guénolé.

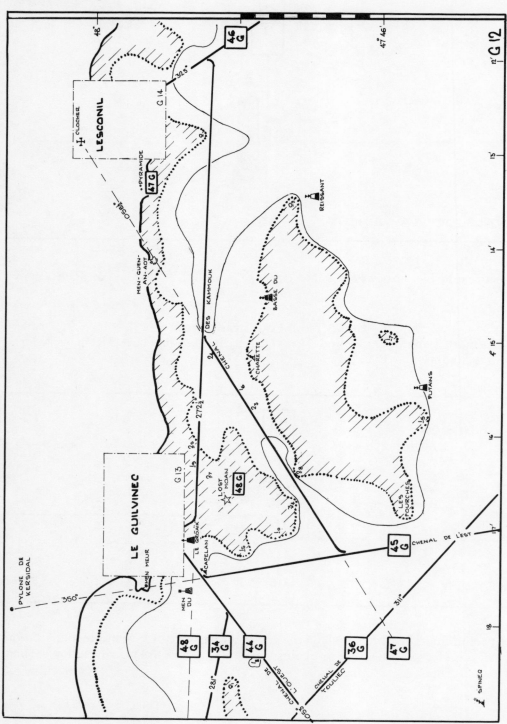

LE GUILVINEC

Here is another commercial ocean fishing harbour, larger than St Guénolé and with a simpler entrance. See chart G12. There are two entrances.

1—Chenal de l'Ouest (1·8m)

First find yourself alongside lit buoy Nevez (CN).

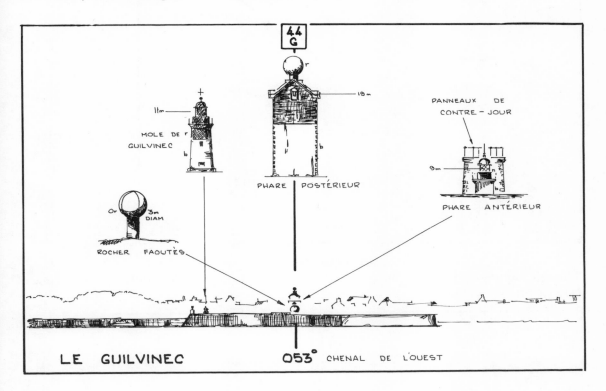

LE GUILVINEC   053° CHENAL DE L'OUEST

44G Two lighthouses in line. For daytime use the harbour officials have been painstaking in providing a pair of enormous oranges. This single mark takes you on to the harbour plan G13 (p.50).

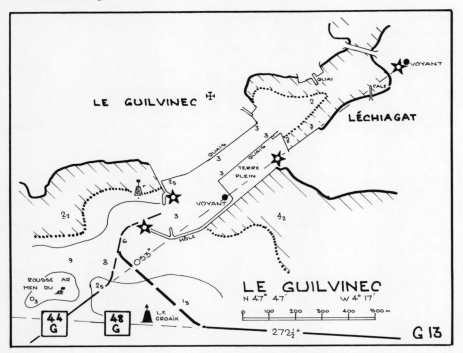

2—Chenal de l'Est (3·7m)

Though slightly deeper than the previous entrance this one is for daytime use only. Chart G12 (p.48).

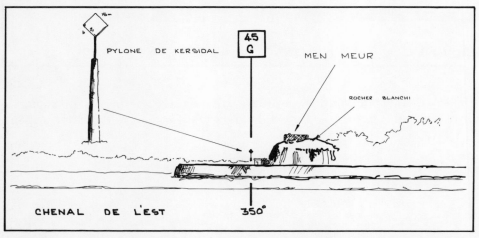

45G Pylone de Kersidal just to the left of Men Meur. This joins the Chenal de l'Ouest immediately west of Capelan stb'd buoy.

Here again the harbourmaster is concerned with commercial fishing but an afloat berth can often be found at the NE end nearby the lifeboat mooring. Drying berths are a-plenty at Léchiagat. Here are all the facilities of a large commercial port.

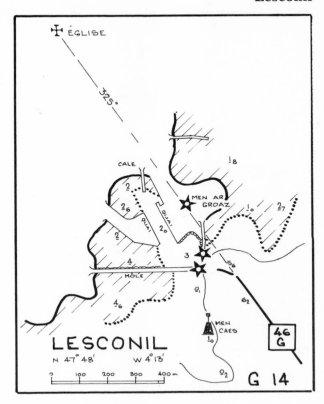

LESCONIL

Another fishing harbour which, since its recent face-lift, has become much busier. The main entrance (which is lit—chart G12 (p.48)) is from the SSE,

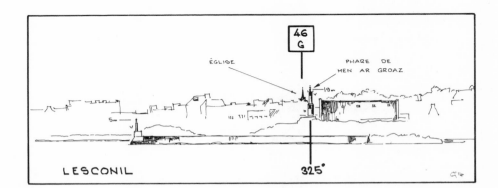

46G Lesconil church × Men ar Groaz light. The harbour plan is on chart G14. A convenient backdoor route is the Chenal des Kammouk. The easiest way is to find the rather difficult lead-in mark from the Chenal de l'Est of Le Guilvinec, see chart G12 (p.48).

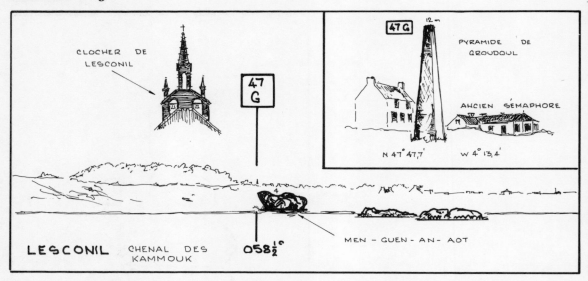

47G Lesconil church spire exactly touching one of a group of rocks on the beach —Men-Guen-an-Aot (*4.0m*). Nearly 2 miles down this mark comes a stern transit

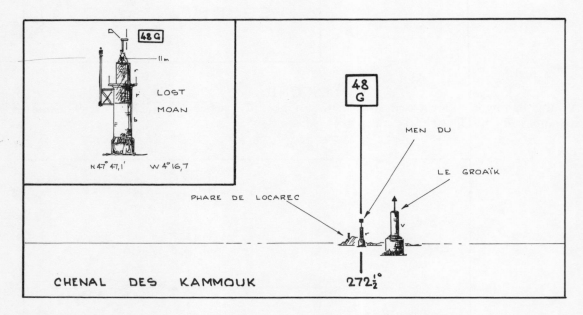

48G three objects in line—Locarec light, Men Du and Le Groaïk *tourelle*. In the same picture I show the nearby Lost Moan light. After a mile you can see the old semaphore and pyramid of Groudoul pictured on 47G. Soon afterwards you join the main channel, see line 46G (p.51). Berths alongside are mostly occupied by fishing boats but the west of inner or outer harbours offer possibilities.

LOCTUDY

Here is the first of the many charming rivers found down this coast. The village at the mouth is called Loctudy and has recently been provided with improved berths for a dozen or more trawlers. From the Anse de Benodet the entrance is clearly seen.

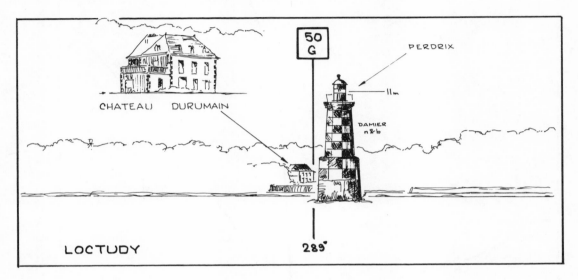

50G a Victorian villa standing alone, Château Durumain, touching the left side of a chequered lighthouse, Perdrix. This line takes you over the bar where there is 0·9m and brings you on to chart G15 (p.54). The breast mark for a turn is

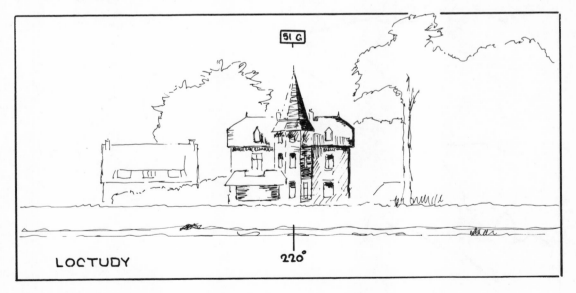

51G a sharp conical roof of a house at 220°. The final mark is

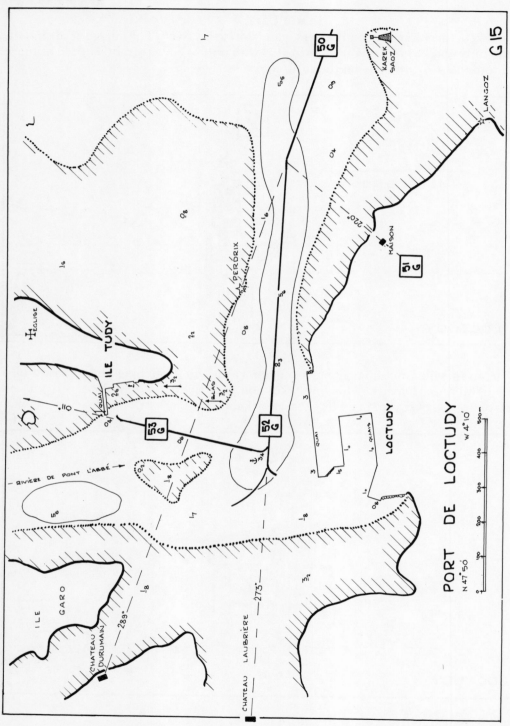

PORT DE LOCTUDY

N 47°50' W 4°10'

G 15

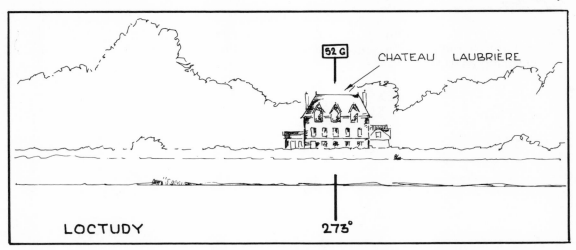

52G Château Laubrière at 273°. I'm sorry about these last two marks not being transits but you are now over the bar and a bit of latitude isn't important.

Since Loctudy is devoted to fishing, anchoring almost anywhere in the river or taking a buoy is necessary.

Ile Tudy

If you want to go across to Ile Tudy without hitting the sand banks take

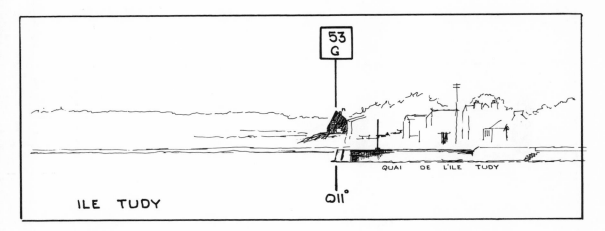

53G an asymmetrical modern gable × end of the quay. The facilities of Ile Tudy are obviously limited.

Pont l'Abbé

It's a most pleasant trip up the river to Pont l'Abbé (3 miles from Loctudy), chart G16. The channel dries about <u>2m</u> in the upper reaches and the quays at Pont l'Abbé are seldom fully occupied. See chart G17.

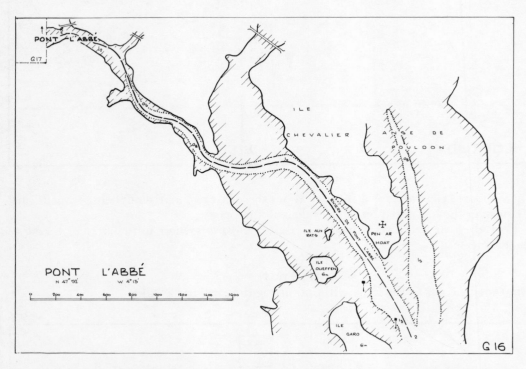

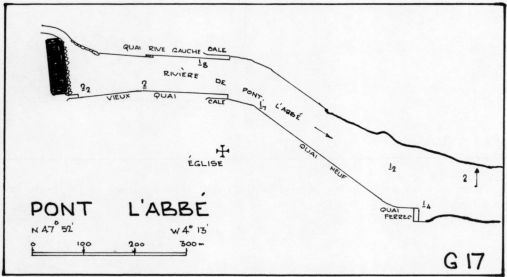

RIVER ODET

Justly popular, the upper reaches of this charming river are still fairly unspoilt. There is little commercial activity, no bar at the river mouth, which can be entered by day or night. The town at the mouth, Benodet, is a noted yachting centre with every facility including a hospitable yacht club, chart G18.

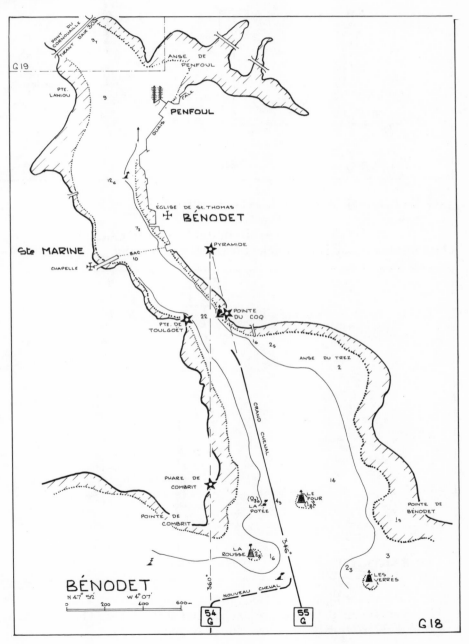

57

French Pilot 3

1—Benodet by Nouveau Chenal

There are 2 channels; the one to take, particularly at night, which leads right into the Anse de Benodet is

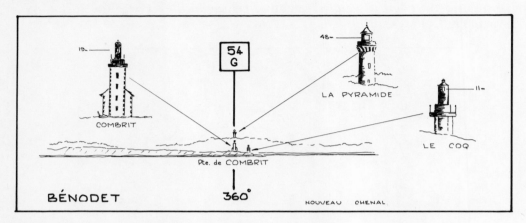

54G La Pyramide lighthouse × Combrit light.

2—Benodet by Grand Chenal

Once inside the bay you can take the river leading lights

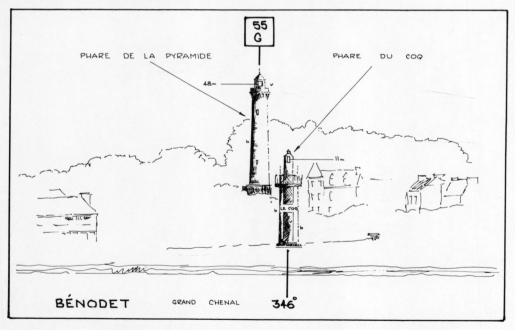

55G La Pyramide light × the Coq light.

The river is deep, the banks are steep to and well marked. There are many buoys, a marina at Penfoul and drying berths alongside in Benodet.

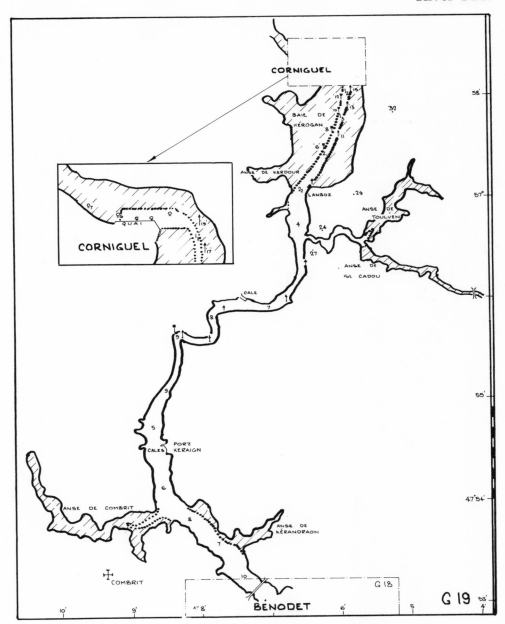

Corniguel

It is an interesting sail up the river but a low bridge now cuts out Quimper for masted boats. However there is a quay at Corniguel, 7 miles from Benodet, shown on chart G19. Except for *sabliers* or an occasional *pinardier* the quays are seldom used. There are no facilities but it is a short mile walk into Quimper.

MOUSTERLIN

I once spent a couple of days sheltering from an easterly gale in this tiny harbour, chart G20, so if I can introduce you to its remote charm,

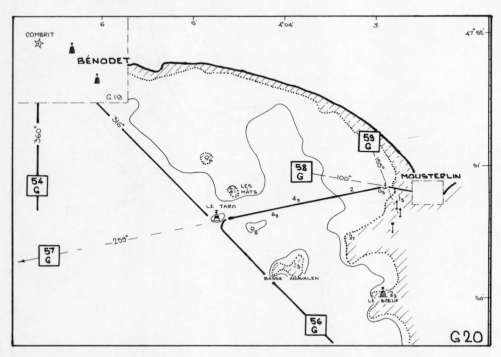

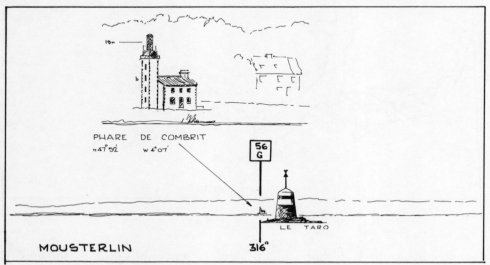

56G is the mark to clear to the west of the Roches de Mousterlin. Combrit light outside Le Taro *tourelle* (CW). The main entrance from Le Taro is a back mark,

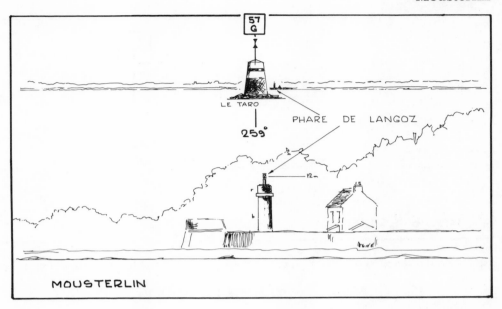

57G Langoz light just to the right of Le Taro. The final mark is

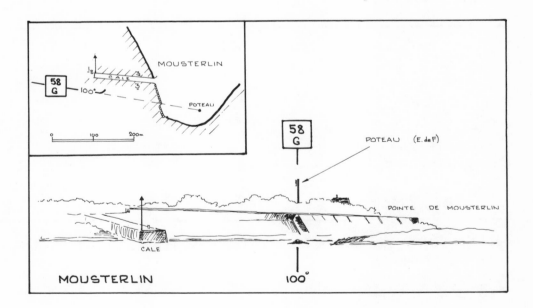

58G a terminal electricity pole × an angle of the sea wall. If you wish to anchor the breast mark is

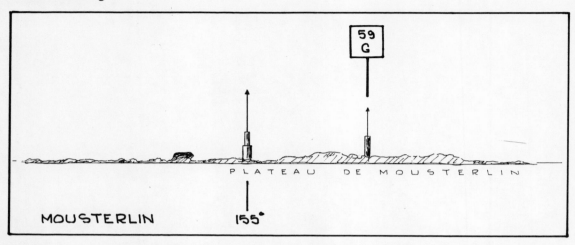

59G two stb'd *balises* in line. You can use either side of the long slip to dry out on firm sand.

BAIE DE LA FORÊT

The next big bay is Baie de la Forêt, see chart G21, and we will start with a sheltered little yachting harbour on the western side.

Beg-Meil

The main mark for the approach from the SE is

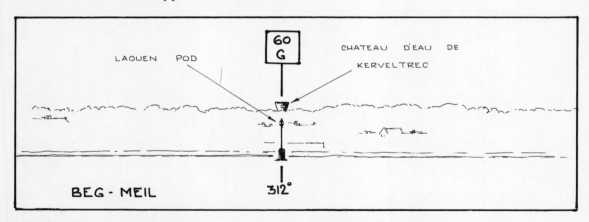

60G Kerveltrec water tower × Laoen Pod *balise* (CE). When a couple of cables from this *balise*, steer north, on to

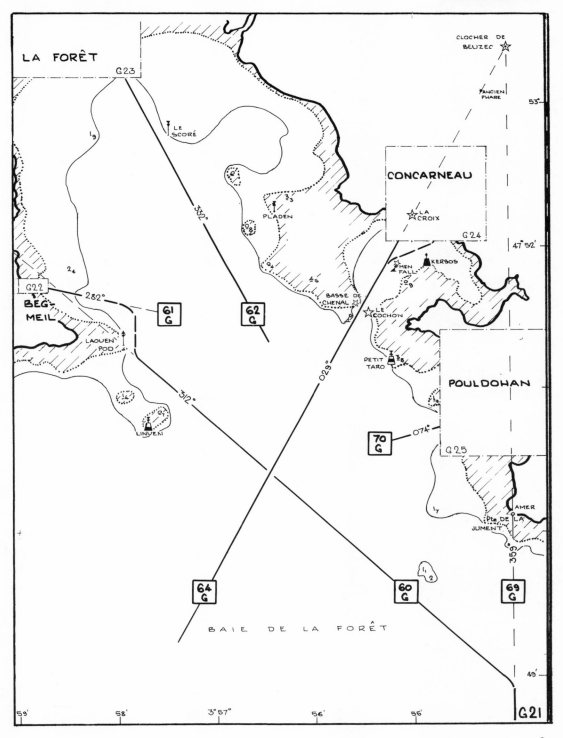

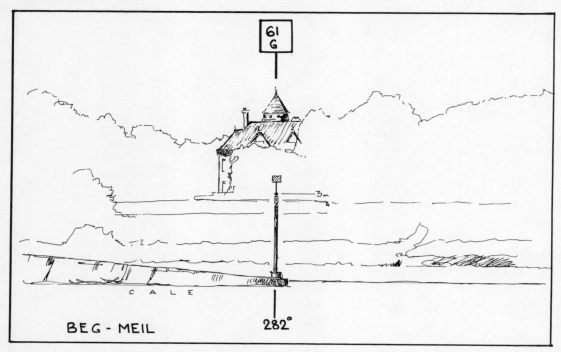

BEG - MEIL

282°

61G a large villa with a conical tower × a lit port *balise* at the end of the slip. Chart G22 shows the drying quays and there are plenty of mooring buoys outside.

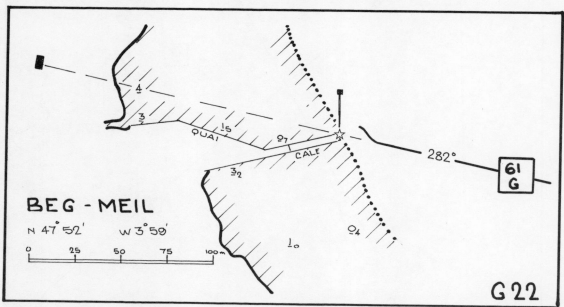

BEG - MEIL

N 47° 52'   W 3° 59'

0   25   50   75   100 m

G 22

At the north of the bay lies one of those enormous marina developments, built in recent years.

La Forêt-Fouesnant

The entrance is well marked chart G.21 (p.63).

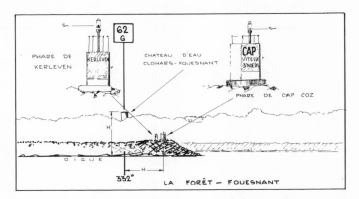

62G Kerleven × Cap Coz lights. By day, however, the small towers are difficult to locate so use Clohars-Fouesnant water tower instead. The marina is shown on chart G23; there are places for 500 boats. Less frequented is the small drying quay ½km north at Strang al Lestrec. Plans are afoot to develop the drying area up to the bridge at La Forêt.

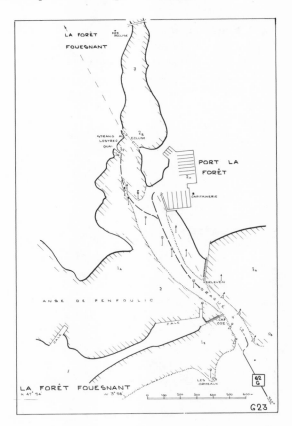

Concarneau

Not only is this France's second largest fishing harbour, but it is an interesting fortified town dating from the fourteenth century. Back to chart G21 (p.63).

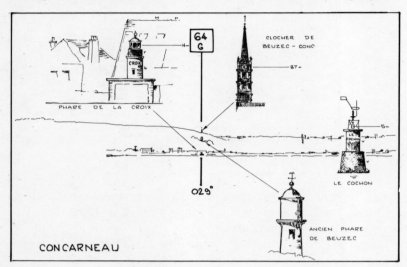

64G Beuzec-Conc church (which has a light on its spire) × La Croix light. Just below the back mark can be seen the disused lighthouse of Beuzec, its top just showing above the trees. By the time you get on to chart G24 the main transit can no longer be seen, so use

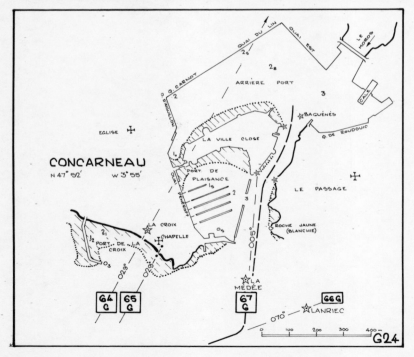

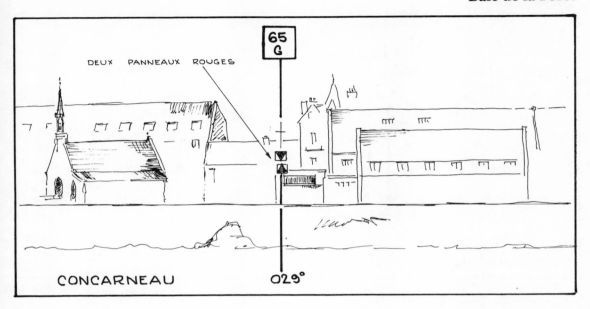

DEUX   PANNEAUX   ROUGES

65
G

CONCARNEAU   029°

65G two red markers in line. These are really the starting line for local yacht racing. As soon as the Men Fall buoy is left to stb'd alter course for

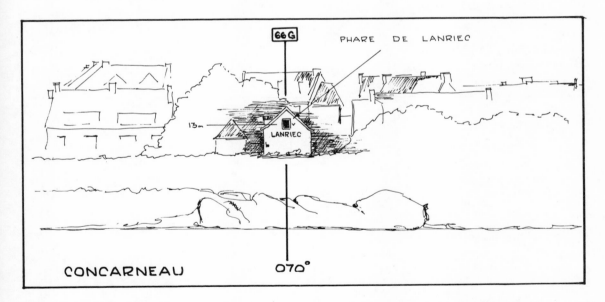

66 G

PHARE   DE   LANRIEC

13m

LANRIEC

CONCARNEAU   070°

66G Lanriec sectored light at 070°. The final mark comes about 2 cables from Lanriec,

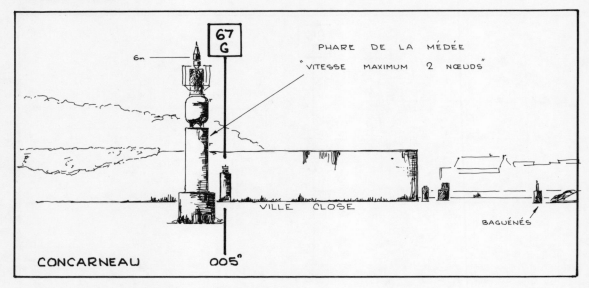

CONCARNEAU   005°

67G the Ville Close light × La Médée light.

The *port de plaisance* is shown on chart G24, the two visitors' pontoons lying parallel to the channel. Though yachts are unwelcome, moorings can sometimes be obtained alongside derelict trawlers in the inner harbour. Port de la Croix is poorly sheltered and therefore little used so drying berths are often free on the east side of the mole.

Pouldohan

The east side of the Baie de la Forêt needs one mark to clear the dangers to the south, see chart G21 (p.63)

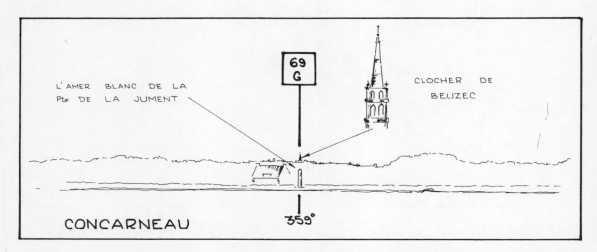

CONCARNEAU   359°

69G Beuzec church × the white *amer* on Pointe de la Jument. There is an interesting little creek, mostly drying, shown on chart G25.

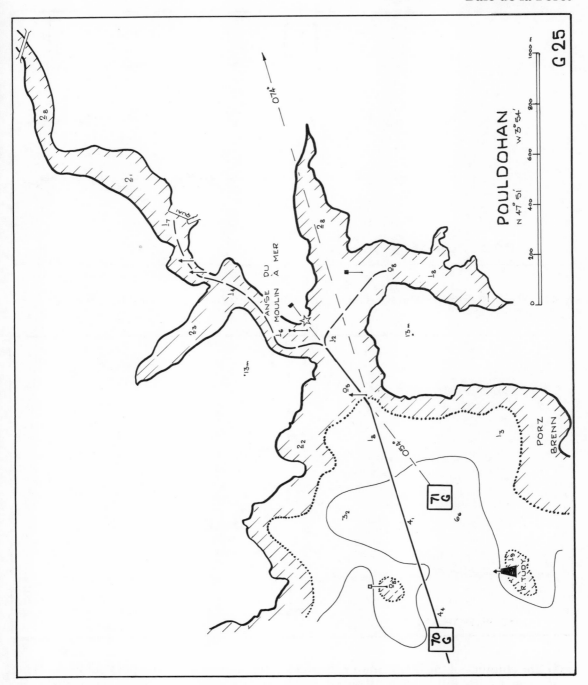

POULDOHAN

N 47° 51'   W 3° 54'

G 25

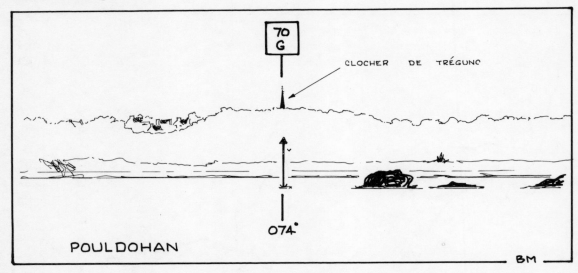

70G Trégunc church × the stb'd *balise* south of the entrance. 50m from the *balise* take

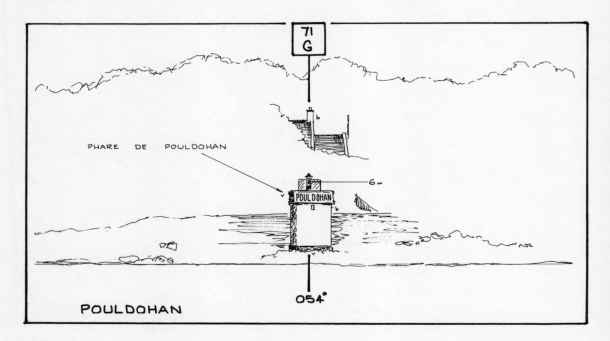

71G the chimney of the house among the trees × the stumpy white light of Pouldohan. The south arm is fairly full of boats all on drying moorings but the north, if you follow the track shown, seems quieter. On the quay there is a prosperous *chantier* where you can buy all kinds of chandlery.

ILES DE GLÉNAN

This archipelago consists of nine islets, one of which has an eighteenth century fort, and is surrounded by reefs covering 30 square miles. Home of the Centre Nautiques des Glénans, the various entrances into this maze of interest are on chart G26. These channels finish at the metropolis of the islands, Ile de St. Nicolas.

1—Chenal des Bluiniers
2—Chenal de Brunec
3—Chenal Pen-a-Men
4—Passage à l'Ouest de Guéotec
5—Chenal de Brilimec
6—Chenal de Ruolh
7—Anchorages

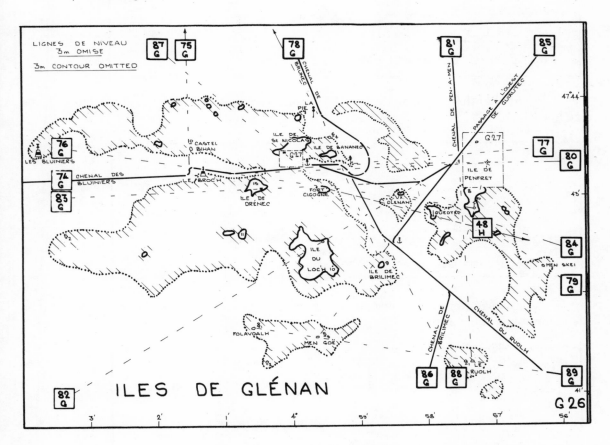

French Pilot 3

1—Chenal des Bluiniers (*o·6m*)

This is the only channel from the west and starts off some 2 cables south of Les Bluiniers *tourelle* (CW).

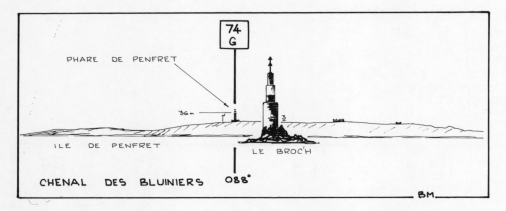

74G Penfret lighthouse just to the left of Le Broc'h *tourelle* (CN). When a cable off this *tourelle* go north

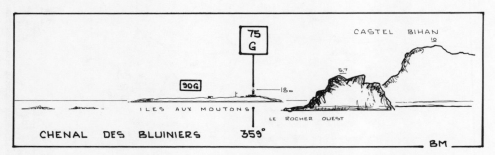

75G Iles aux Moutons lighthouse to the left of the west rock of Castel Bihan (*5·7m*). This is held for only a cable until

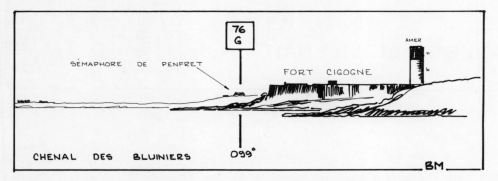

76G the disused semaphore on Penfret just to the left of Fort Cigogne. After 4 cables take

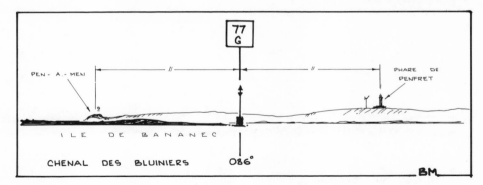

77G the Ile de Bananec *balise* (CE) × midway between Penfret lighthouse and the most northerly rock of Penfret, Pen-a-Men (*9·0m*). This leads into the central anchorage off Ile de St Nicolas.

2—Chenal de Brunec (0·7m)

This, from the NNW, is the shortest channel.

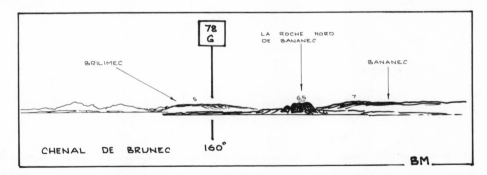

78G Brilimec, a low island 5m high, to the left of the north head of Bananec. This mark leaves La Pie *balise* (*isolée*) less than a cable to stb'd, and when abreast of it take

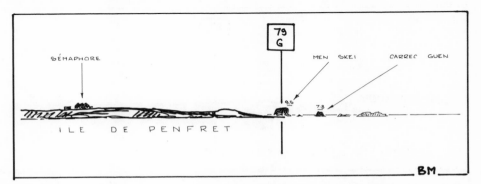

79G Men Skei, nearly 3 miles away (*9·5m*) × the south end of Ile Penfret. When abreast of the Bananec *balise* (CE) make a handrail a cable off to the east and south, until

73

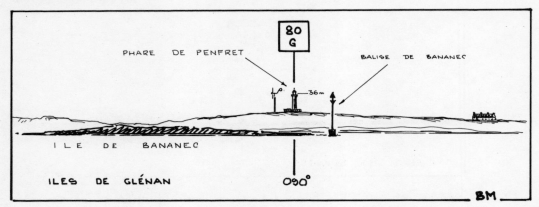

80G Penfret lighthouse ✕ the same Bananec beacon, which leads to the Ile de St Nicolas anchorage.

3—Chenal Pen-a-Men (0·6m)

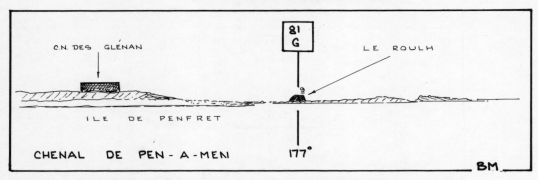

81G Le Ruolh open to the right of the SW point of Penfret. When a cable past the north point of Penfret, look for

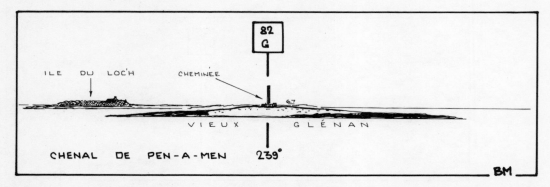

82G the chimney on Ile Loc'h ✕ Le Vieux Glénan (*6·7m*). This is a flat sandy island.

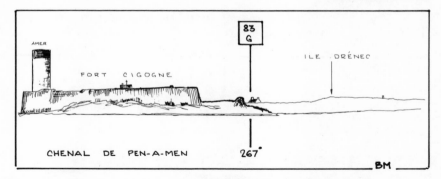

83G The right hand house on Drénec × a pointed rock to the right of Fort Cigogne.

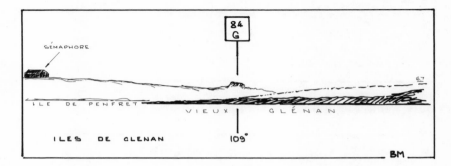

84G The hummock to the right of the semaphore on Penfret × the left of Le Vieux Glénan, which takes you to the anchorage.

4—Passage à l'Ouest de Guéotec (0·6m)

This channel is not so much an entrance as one of the channels from north to south through the archipelago. The exit south of this one is the Chenal de Ruolh.

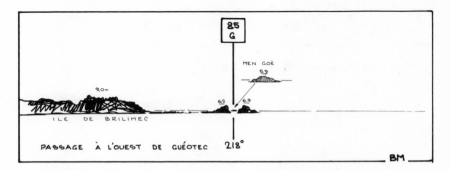

85G Men Goë (*5·9m*) midway between the two heads of rock to the right of Ile de Brilimec. This takes you to one of the anchorages later described.

French Pilot 3

5—Chenal de Brilimec (7·0m)

This channel from the south starts off with two unambiguous man-made objects,

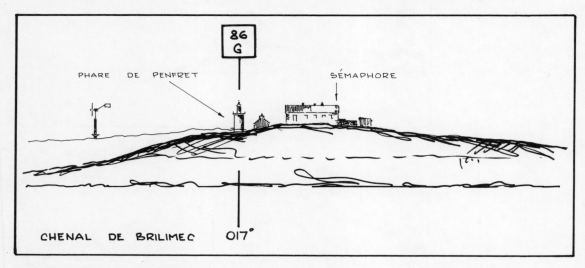

86G Penfret light to the left of the semaphore, until

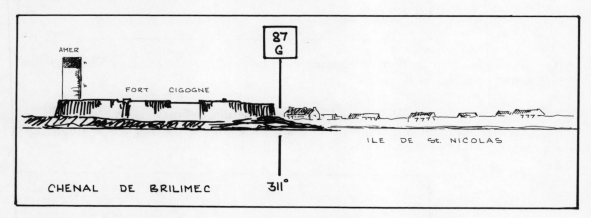

87G the big house on Ile de St Nicolas ✕ the right hand side of Fort Cigogne.

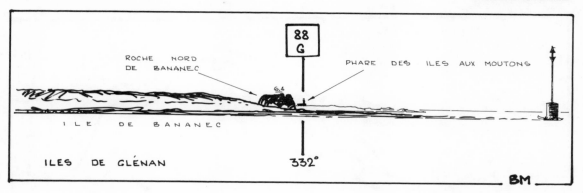

88G The Iles aux Moutons light ✕ the north rock of Bananec (*6·4m*). When 2 cables off the Bananec *balise* (CE) follow view 84G (p.75) which takes you to the anchorage.

6—Chenal de Ruolh (5·0m)

This is the normal channel from the east.

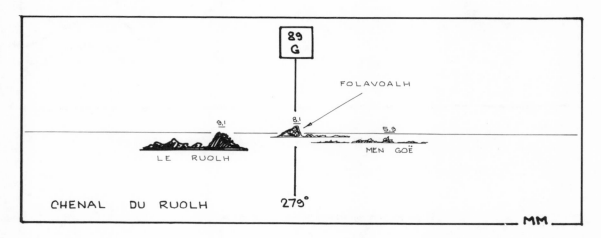

89G Folavoalh (*8·1m*) just to the right of Le Ruolh (*9·1m*). About ½ mile before Le Ruolh take view 87G, Chenal de Brilimec.

7—Anchorages

The Centre Nautique have provided mooring buoys for their own sailing schools, which can be used by visitors. They are 1 cable NW of Bananec, just north of Ile Drénec, Fort Cigogne and Ile de Brilimec. On chart G27 (p.78) the two anchorages off Penfret are shown, near the slip at Pors Niguer and south of the lighthouse. Ile de St Nicolas is shown on the same page. A line of mooring buoys has been laid south of the quay. This is a good place to show

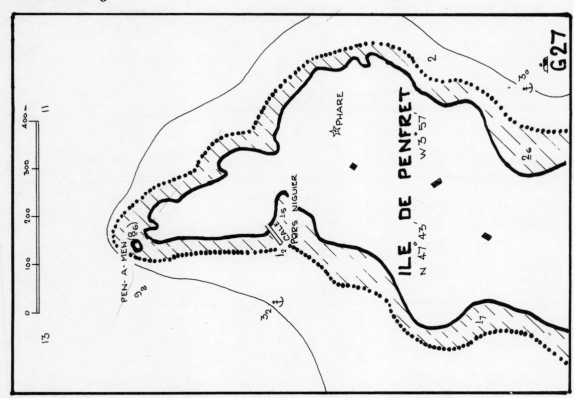

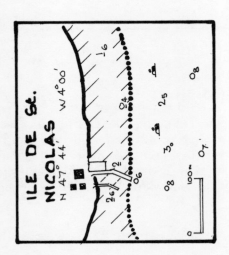

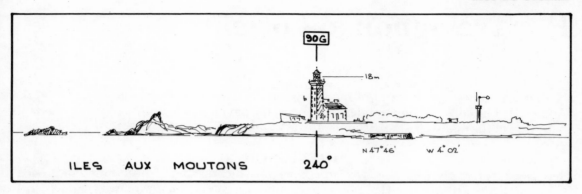

90G a view of Ile aux Moutons light.

H   Trèvignon to Lorient

The next 25 miles are the land of moors, mountains and legend—the Round Table, the Vannetais. The cliffs provide wonderful scenery, the navigation is simple and we come soon to the first of the many off-shore islands, Ile de Groix.

TRÈVIGNON

Here is a surprisingly well sheltered little harbour which has lately been much improved. The approaches are on chart H1 and the harbour on chart H2. There are two channels both covered at night by the sectored lighthouse. The simplest is from the south.

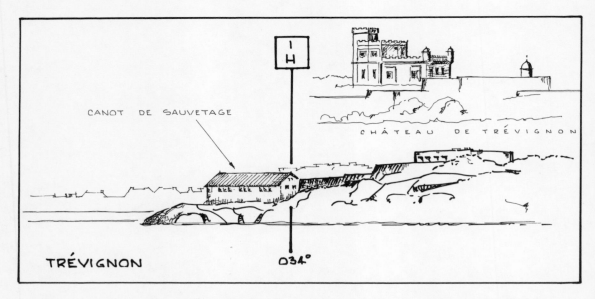

1H The right-hand gable of the lifeboat station ✕ the left wall of Château de Trèvignon. Trèvignon Point is steep to and can be followed round into the harbour a cable off. The western approach has rocks close on either side.

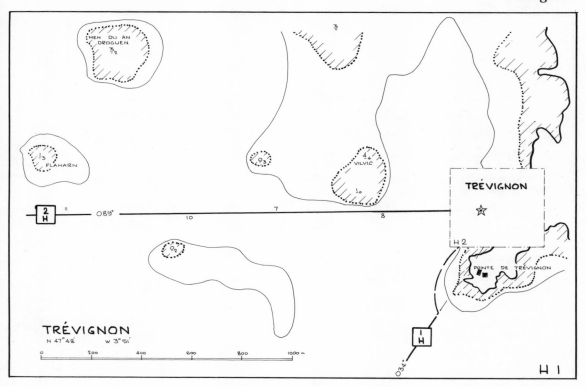

TRÉVIGNON
N 47° 48'   W 3° 51'

H 1

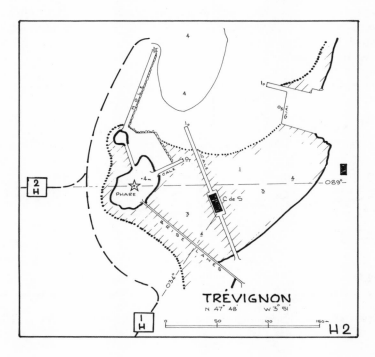

TRÉVIGNON
N 47° 48'   W 3° 51'

H 2

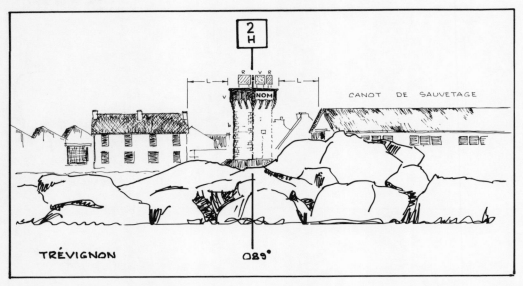

TRÉVIGNON   089°

2H The lighthouse × exactly midway between the left-hand gable of the lifeboat station and the right-hand gable of a prominent house with three chimneys. When you are near enough to see it, the lantern of the lighthouse can be fitted midway between the glass screens which make the sectors.

RAGUÉNÈS

A couple of miles to the east there are two low islets, Ile Verte and Raguénès. Just NE of the latter there is a most sheltered anchorage in which many moorings have been provided for fishing and pleasure boats, shown on chart H3. The safest approach is from the east and to clear the outliers of Ile Verte use

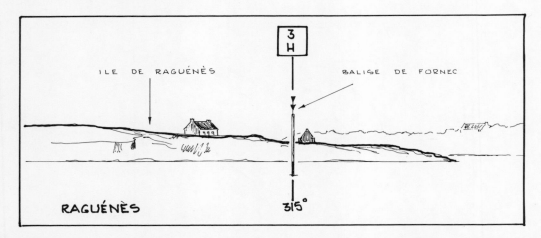

RAGUÉNÈS   315°

3H the right-hand house on Raguénès × the *balise* (CS). Useful for recognition are the two *amers* of

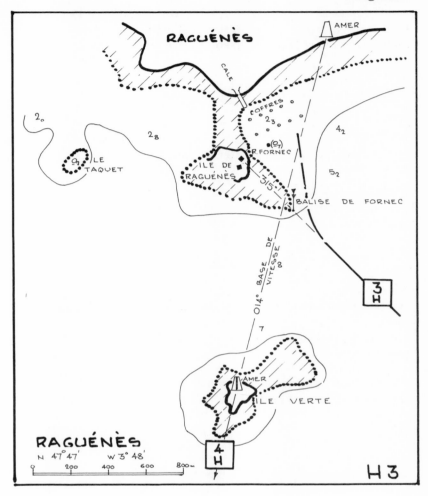

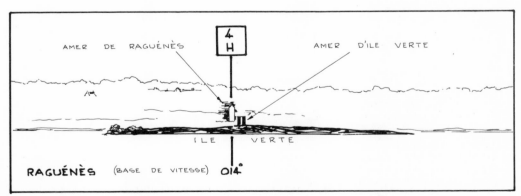

4H the alignment for the measured distance for which see chart H27 (p.117).

AVEN and BELON RIVERS

Two of the prettiest rivers in this indented coast, they have numerous sheltered and deep anchorages, chart H4. The harbours are taken in this order:

1—Port Manech
2—Kerdruc and Rosbras
3—Pont-Aven
4—Belon and Lanriot

1—Port Manech

A very sheltered and deep water anchorage at the river entrance with convenient quays. For recognition

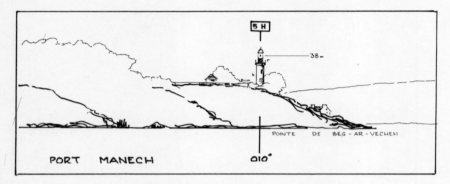

5H the main lighthouse of Port Manech. Its sectored light clears all dangers into the river. Clearance of the rocks off Pointe de Beg-ar-Vechen is given by

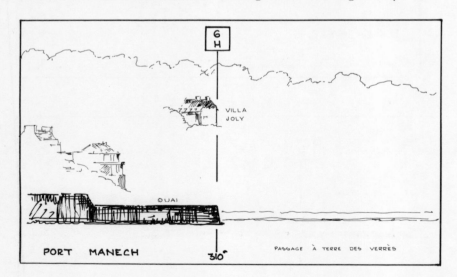

6H the Villa Joly × the end of the quay. This same mark can be used for entering the bay from the SE between Les Verrès and the shore. The harbour is on chart H5.

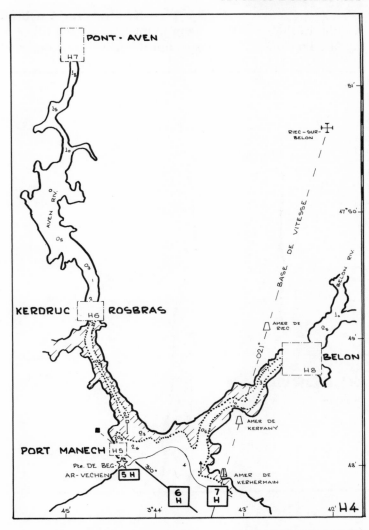

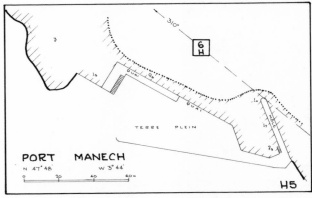

2—Kerdruc and Rosbras

A mile up the river these twin hamlets face each other from either bank; chart H6 gives details. The quays can be used but there are many moorings in the river.

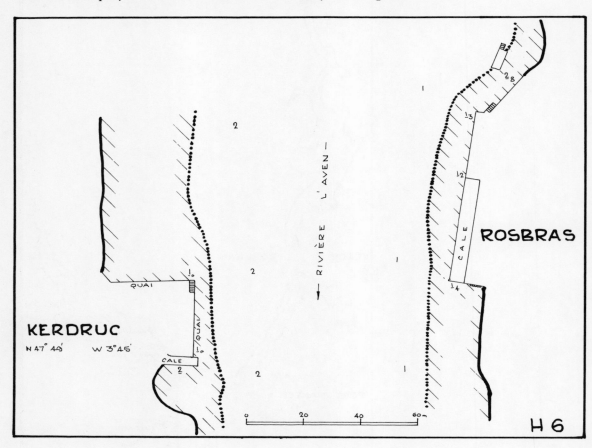

3—Pont-Aven

Pontaven, ville de renom,
Quinze moulins, quatorze maisons.

This couplet used to describe this snug little town at the head of navigation. Paul Gauguin who died in 1903 started the Pont-Aven school of painting and there is a museum containing many of his works. Chart H7 shows the drying quays where there is normally ample room.

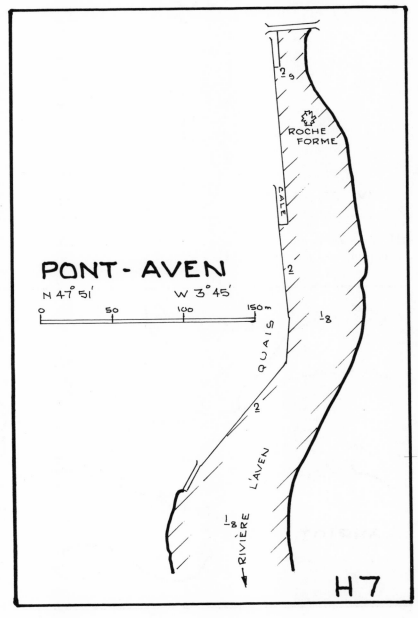

4—Belon and Lanriot

Apart from the world famous oysters there is little at Belon, which is a mile from the river mouth. But it is a beautiful river to explore and the quay at Lanriot, see chart H8, has recently been improved.

Returning to the bay, here is another transit,

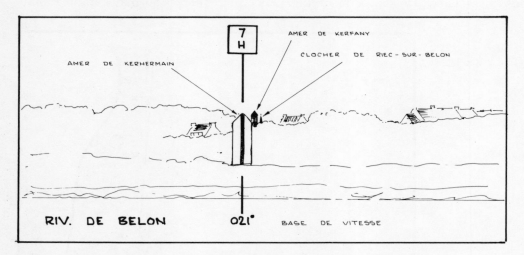

7H Riec-sur-Belon church, *amer* of Kerfany and *amer* of Kerhermain in line, the marks for a measured distance, see chart H27 (p.117).

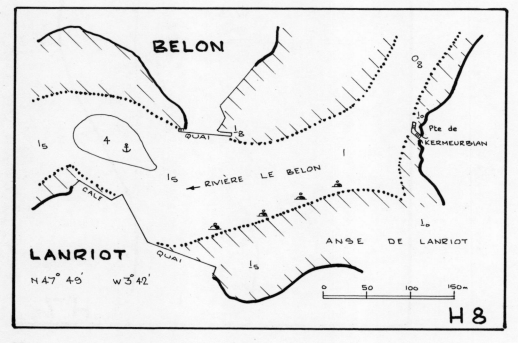

BRIGNEAU

Here is a seldom used little harbour, a disused relic of the sardine fishing era, chart H9. The white sector of the light clears the several dangers but in daytime use

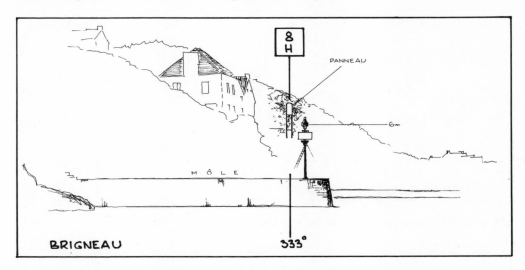

BRIGNEAU

333°

8H a white panel just to the left of the light at the end of the quay. Two or three fishing boats use the *arrière port* but there is usually plenty of room.

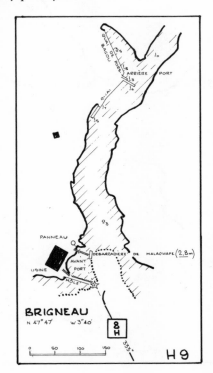

BRIGNEAU

N 47°47'   W 3°40'

H 9

89

MERRIEN

An acute bend keeps the swell away from this tiny drying creek, chart H10. The entrance mark is

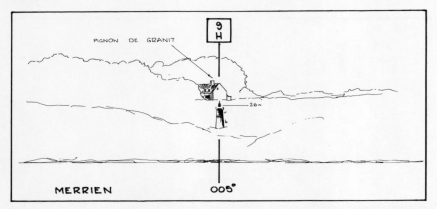

9H a granite farmhouse × the lighthouse, which is also the visible sector of the light.

DOËLAN

With nine quays, a breakwater and two lighthouses, surely Doëlan is worth more than the half-dozen fishing boats which use it, chart H11?

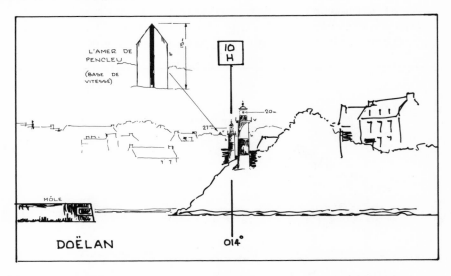

10H shows the main alignment which, with the *amer* of Pencleu, form part of the measured distance, chart H27 (p.117).

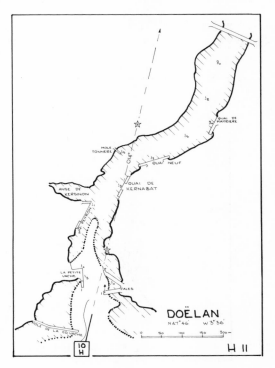

LE POULDU

This harbour is seldom visited because of the bar at its entrance. Fortunately this rarely moves. The estuary is shown on chart H12 and because the river Quimperlé is tidal for 7 miles the currents on the ebb reach 6 knots. If you have enough power, it is as well to enter as soon as you like after low water though naturally not with any swell. For lack of names I have given the navigational aids numbers, so we will start with

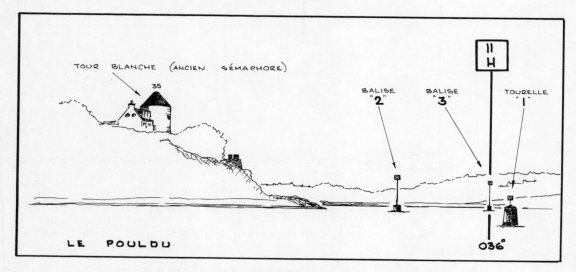

11H *balise* '3' × port *tourelle* '1'. Make a handrail east-about and leave *tourelle* '1' and *balise* '2' 25m to port. Follow the track shown on chart H12 until past *balise* '3' when you take a back mark,

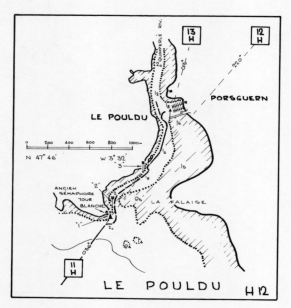

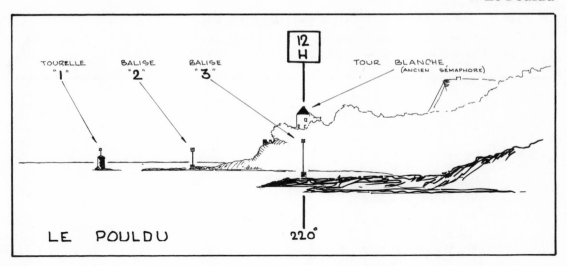

12H the old semaphore × *balise* '*3*'. The final mark, leading to a small *port de plaisance* at Porsguern is

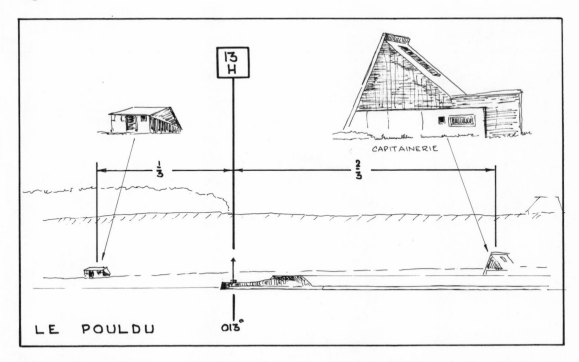

13H the stb'd *balise* at the end of the breakwater between two buildings in the ratio shown. The marina offers limited facilities and only in high summer. The nearest shops are across the river at Le Pouldu. There are deep water moorings up the river Laïta as far as the bridge at Beg-Nenez.

French Pilot 3

LE COURÉGANT

Don't expect too much from chart H13 but at least there is a miniature quay to dry out alongside. The mark is

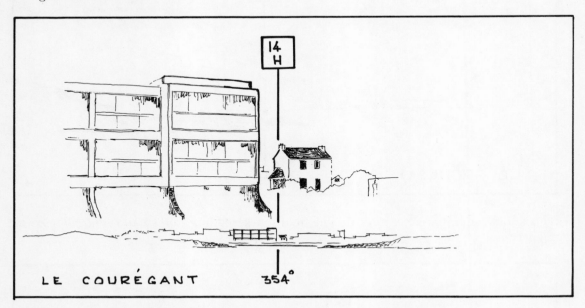

LE COURÉGANT   354°

14H the left gable of a white house ✕ the right of a long block of apartments.

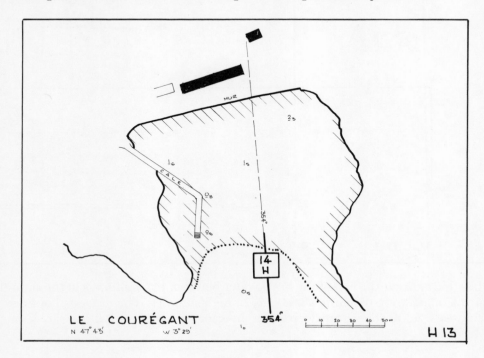

LE COURÉGANT
N 47°43'   W 3°29'   354°   H 13

POINTE DU TALUT

This area is strictly called the Coureau de Groix and there are three interesting little harbours before making our way across to Ile de Groix, chart H14.

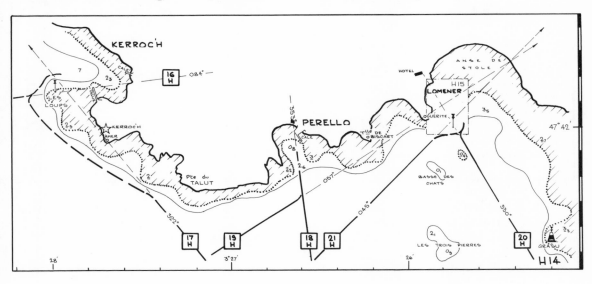

Kerroc'h

There are several rocks in the approach and the line leading south of Les Soeurs is

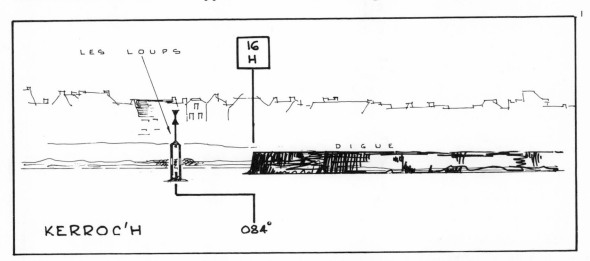

16H the end of the *digue* × the right of Les Loups *balise* (CW). Allow a cable off this tripod-based *balise*. If coming from the SE you can use another of those alignments for measured distance.

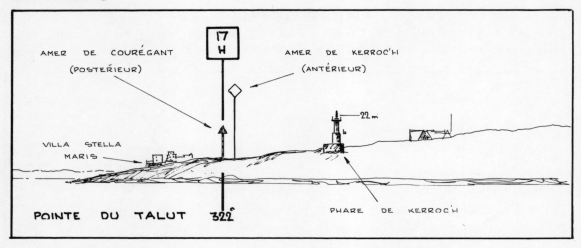

AMER DE COURÉGANT
(POSTÉRIEUR)

AMER DE KERROC'H
(ANTÉRIEUR)

17
H

22 m

VILLA STELLA
MARIS

POINTE DU TALUT 322°

PHARE DE KERROC'H

17H The *amer* of Courégant × the *amer* of Kerroc'h which keeps you clear of the rocks near Pointe du Talut until it is time to turn for Les Loups.

Perello

This is a small, but quite well sheltered, enclosed sandy bay with a slip. The easiest entrance is from the south, take

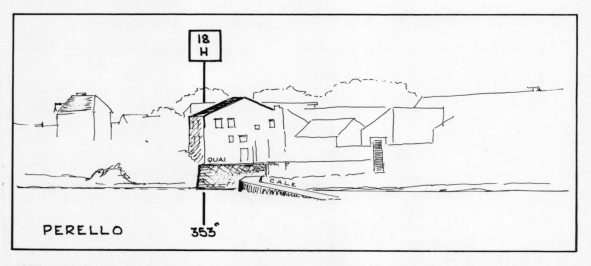

18
H

QUAI

CALE

PERELLO 353°

18H the left side of a large warehouse × the root of the quay. If coming from the west don't tangle with the rocks off Fort du Talut the clearance mark for which is

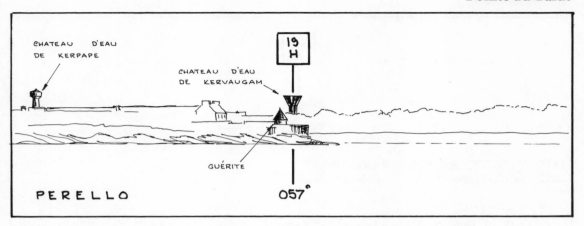

19H the water tower of Kervaugam × a conical watch house at Lomener.

Lomener

Not only does this have a sheltered area of non-drying moorings but a reasonable sized quay to dry out against. The easiest entrance is by Grasu *tourelle* (CS) Chart H14 (p.95).

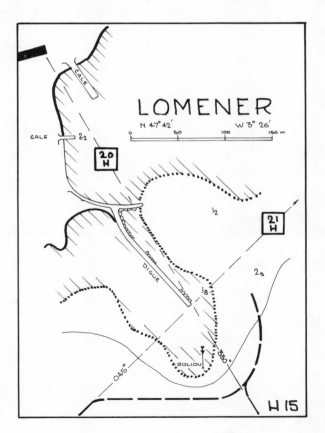

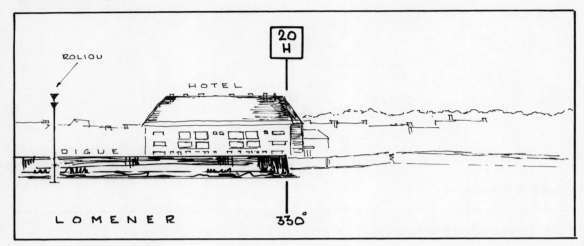

20H The right of a vast hotel ✕ the end of the outer breakwater. Chart H15 (p.97) shows the harbour. From the SW and to clear inside Les Trois Pierres and Basse des Chats take

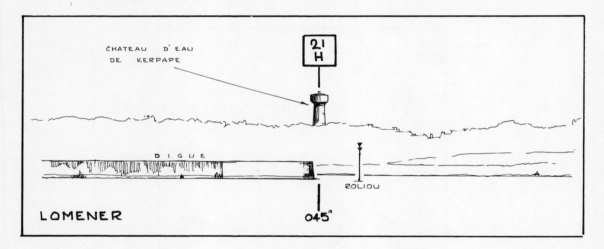

21H the water tower of Kerpape ✕ the end of the same breakwater.

ILE DE GROIX
Once the home of Morgan-le-Fée, Cornish half-sister to King Arthur, this compact little island is a dormitory for the commuters from Lorient.

Port Tudy
This is the harbour of Le Bourg. Formally important for tunny fishing, it has its half dozen fishing boats, a new marina and the terminus for the Lorient ferries, chart H16. The entrance is straightforward but to clear a shoal off Pointe du Spernec use

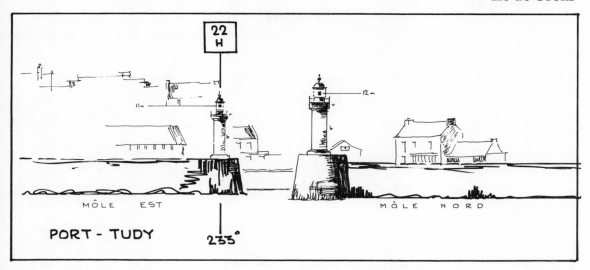

MÔLE EST   MÔLE NORD

PORT - TUDY   233°

22H the two entrance lighthouses no more open than shown. The harbour gets very crowded but there are several mooring buoys in the *avant port*. Every facility.

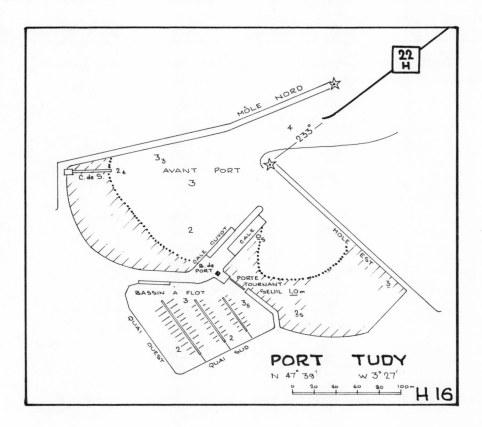

PORT TUDY

N 47° 39'   W 3° 27'

0 20 40 60 80 100 m

H 16

99

French Pilot 3

Port Lay

Half a mile to the west there is a much less popular drying harbour on chart H17. To avoid a shoal in the entrance use

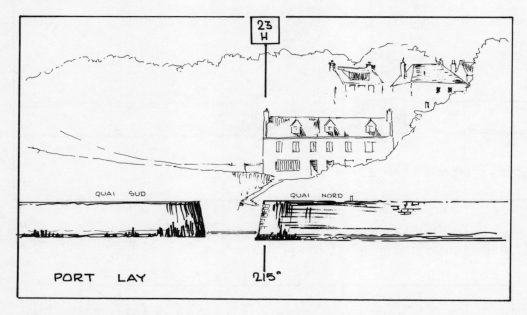

23H the left chimney of a large house with three dormers × the end of the north quay. If the shop at Kermario is out of stock, it is a kilometre walk to Le Bourg.

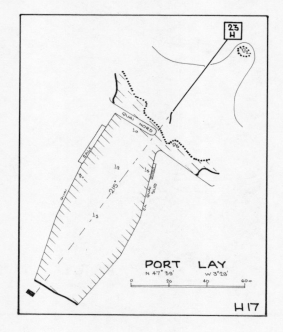

PORT LAY
N 47° 39'   W 3° 28'

H17

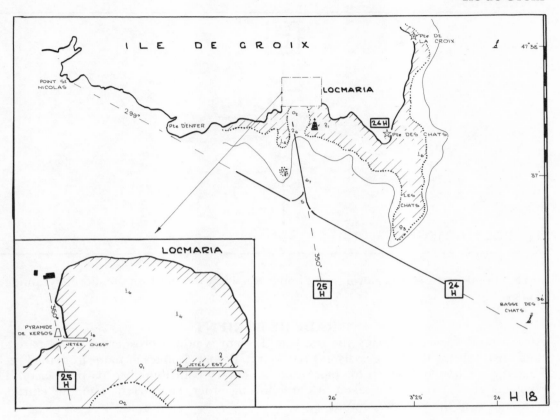

Locmaria

There is a pleasant little harbour on the SE coast though open to the SW. The approaches are on chart H18. To clear Les Chats or the rocks to the west of the entrance use

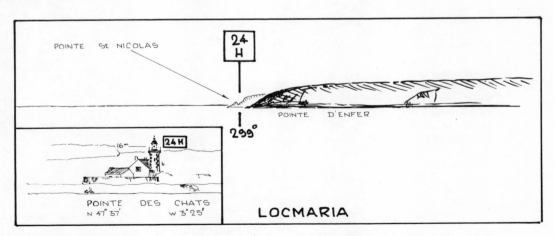

24H the Pointe St Nicolas visible outside Pointe d'Enfer. The final mark is

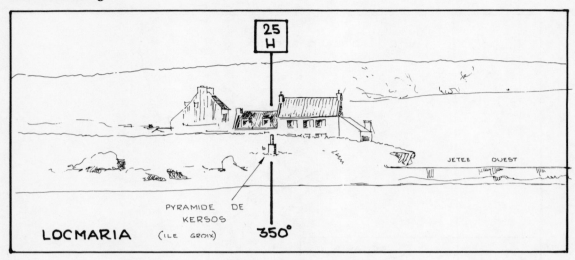

25H a break in the roof of a prominent house × a white daymark on the shore, Pyramide de Kersos.

RADE DE LORIENT

Almost totally levelled during the last war, Lorient is now a prosperous naval base and dockyard. It is the third largest fishing harbour in France. It takes its name from the French East India Company which for more than a century contributed to its prosperity. The channels and harbours are taken in the following order, chart H19. The four entrances terminate near the Port de Commerce.

    1—Passe de l'Ouest
    2—Passe de l'Ouest (Grasu)
    3—Passe de l'Ouest (Pierre d'Orge)
    4—Passe du Sud
    5—Larmor
    6—Kernével
    7—Lorient, Bassin à Flot
    8—Pen-Mané
    9—Ile St Michel
    10—Locmiguélic
    11—Port Louis
    12—Locmalo
    13—Ban-Gâvres
    14—Pen-er-Bed
    15—Hennebont

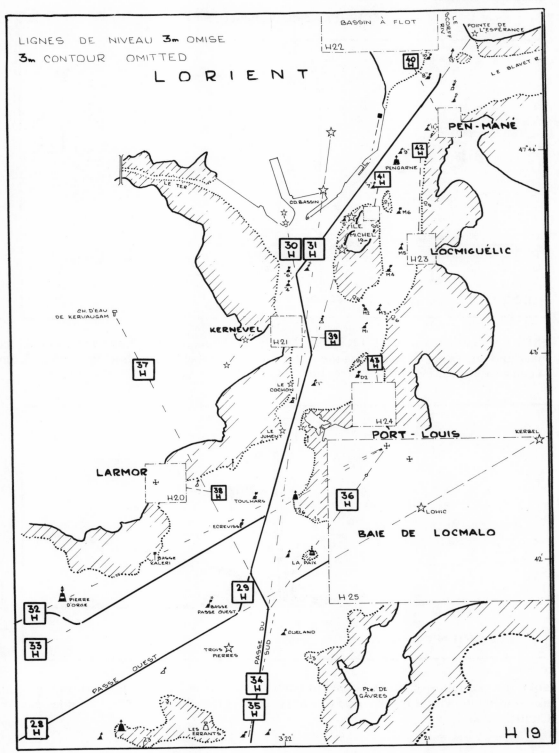

LIGNES DE NIVEAU **3m** OMISE

3m CONTOUR OMITTED

L O R I E N T

BASSIN À FLOT

H22

POINTE DE L'ESPÉRANCE

LE BLAVET R.

40 H

PEN-MANÉ

47°44

42 H

PENGARNE

41 H

M6

ÎLE St MICHEL

LOCMIGUÉLIC

H23

M5

CD. BASSIN

30 H   31 H

M4

M3

M2

M1

CH. D'EAU DE KERVAUGAM

KERNEVEL

H21

39 H

43°

37 H

43 H

D2

LE COCHON

H24

PORT - LOUIS

KERBEL

LE JUMENT

LARMOR

H20

36 H

LOHIC

38 H

TOULHARS

BAIE DE LOCMALO

42′

ÉCREVISSE

BASSE KALERI

LA PAIX

PIERRE D'ORGE

29 H

32 H

BASSE PASSE OUEST

GUELAND

Pte. DE GÂVRES

33 H

TROIS PIERRES

PASSE OUEST

PASSE DU SUD

34 H

35 H

28 H

LES ERRANTS

H 19

103

1—Passe de l'Ouest (5·2m)

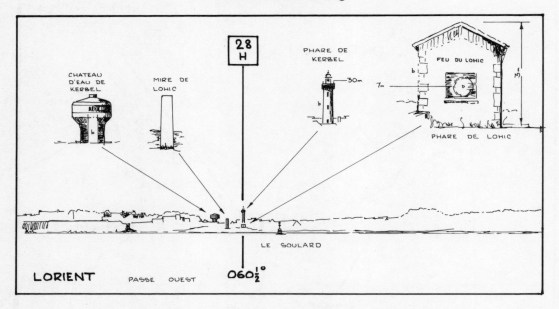

CHATEAU
D'EAU DE
KERBEL

MIRE DE
LOHIC

28
H

PHARE DE
KERBEL

FEU DU LOHIC

PHARE DE LOHIC

LE SOULARD

LORIENT   PASSE OUEST   060½°

28H The lighthouse of Kerbel × Lohic. This is easy by night but by day an almost identical mark and one easier to pick out is the water tower of Kerbel × the white daymark of Lohic. When a cable past Les Trois Pierres light take

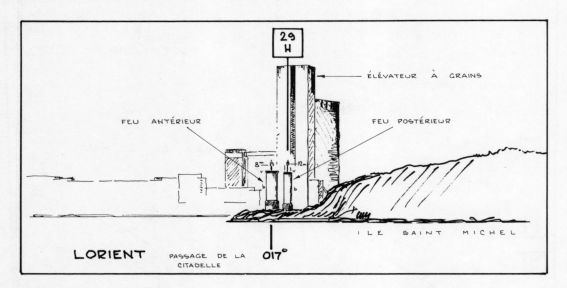

29
H

ÉLÉVATEUR À GRAINS

FEU ANTÉRIEUR

FEU POSTÉRIEUR

ILE SAINT MICHEL

LORIENT   PASSAGE DE LA
CITADELLE   017°

29H the two lights of Ile St Michel in line (Passage de la Citadelle). An enormous grain elevator, white with a black stripe down its centre, gives the clue. When 3 cables past the Citadelle take

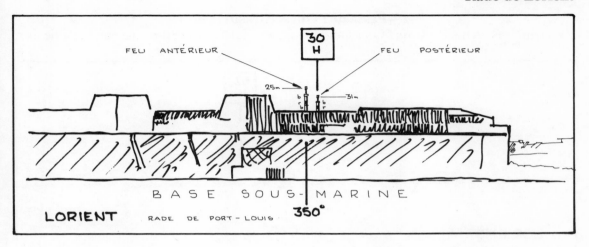

30H two lights in line above the submarine base. When nearly abreast of the lit stb'd buoy Banc du Turc, look behind you for

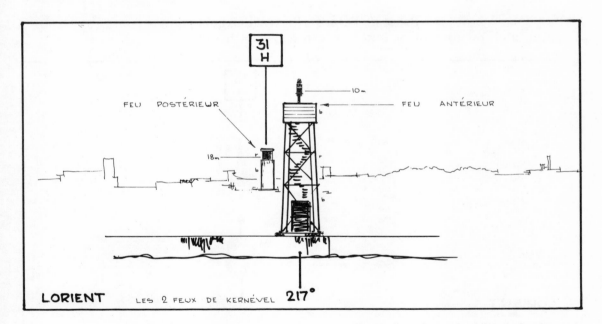

31H the two lights of Kernével in line.

2—Passe de l'Ouest (Grasu) (5·2m)

As a tributary to the Passe de l'Ouest and to take you safely inside the Basse de la Paille use

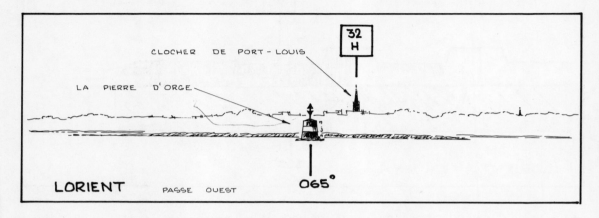

32H Port Louis church × La Pierre d'Orge *tourelle* (CE).

3—Passe de l'Ouest (Pierre d'Orge) (3·9m)

If tacking and you want all the water you can get , a northern limit is

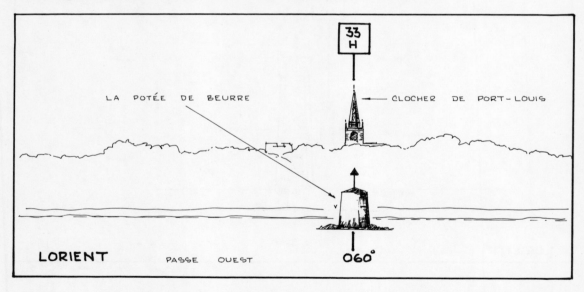

33H Port Louis church × La Potée de Beurre stb'd *tourelle* which can be used until view 29H, Passage de la Citadelle (p.104).

4—Passe du Sud (4·5m)

This is fine at night time and is

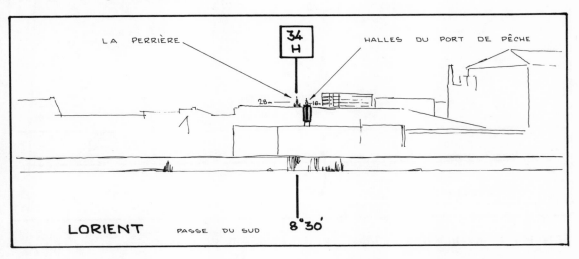

34H La Perrière light × the light on the fishmarket. By day it is well-nigh impossible as the tiny light structures, even though they have topmarks, are difficult to see at 3½ miles. Instead I offer

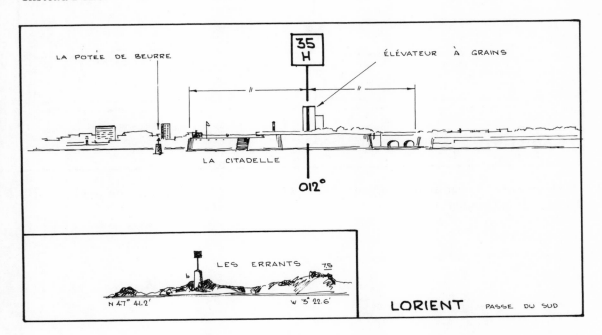

35H that enormous grain elevator midway between the left and right sides of the Citadelle which serves equally well. When past Le Goëland stb'd buoy look for a breast mark

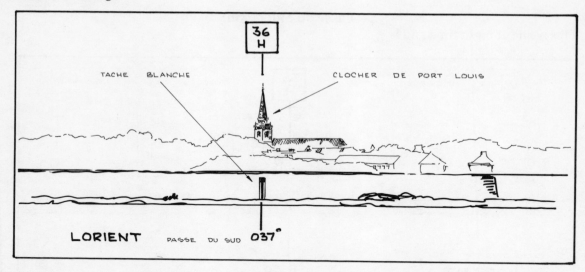

36H Port Louis church × a white mark on the sea-wall. When this comes up steer for

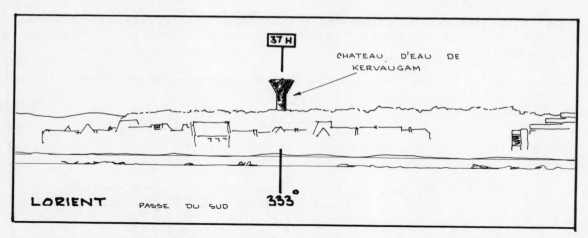

37H the water tower at Kervaugam about 333°. Two cables later come on to view 29H, Passage de la Citadelle (p.104).

5—Larmor

Chart H20 shows this busy little drying harbour entered between two *balises*. One mark serves

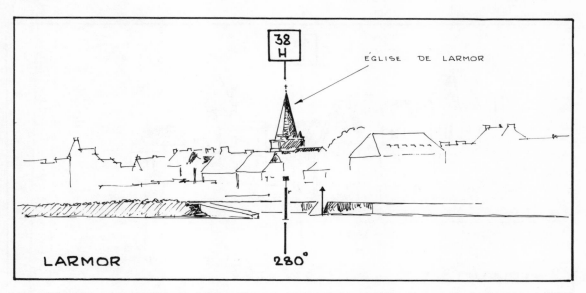

38H the church spire × the port entrance *balise*.

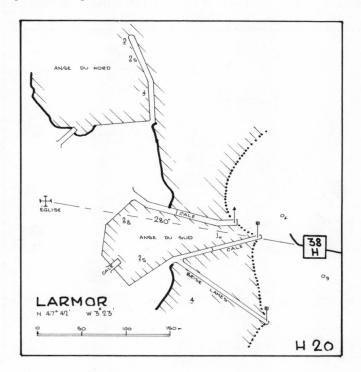

6—Kernével

Whilst I show the slip, this is difficult to use and there is a vast area of afloat moorings immediately to the north, chart H21. A useful mark is

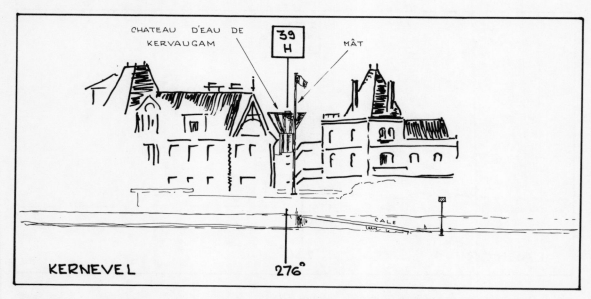

39H Kervaugam water tower (striped) × the flagstaff outside the yacht club.

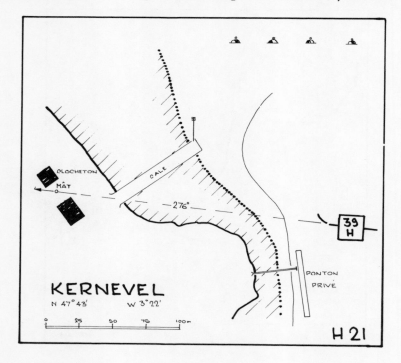

7—Lorient, Bassin à Flot

Chart H22 shows the entrance to what was the Bassin du Commerce. It is now a yacht marina with a lock gate and there is only room in the *avant port* for boats waiting to use the lock. The gates open by day only, 1 hour before or after high water at springs, ½ hour before or after at neaps. The River Scorff is a military area and therefore prohibited for all craft.

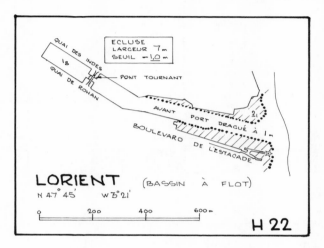

8—Pen-Mané

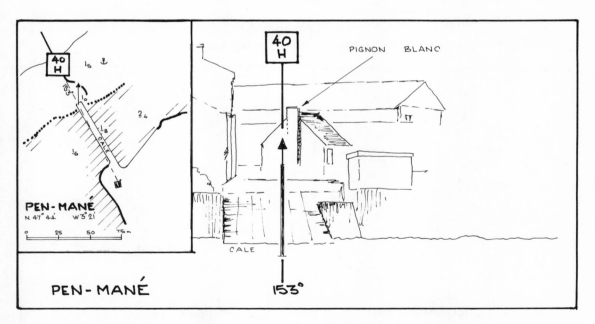

40H shows the mark used by the ferry men, a white gable × the stb'd *balise* at the end of the slip. This is in constant use by the Lorient ferries.

9—Ile St Michel

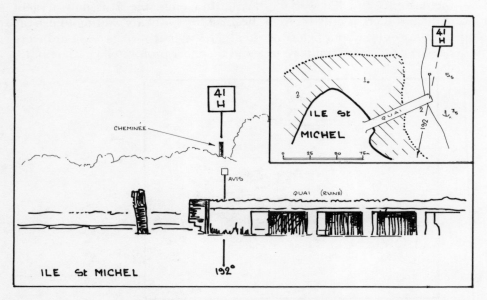

41H A chimney × a notice board leads you between mud banks to a partly ruined quay. It's a military area but since the notice on the quay was probably signed by Napoleon, it is a favourite place for picnics.

10—Locmiguélic

Chart H23 gives details of this ferry harbour and the mark

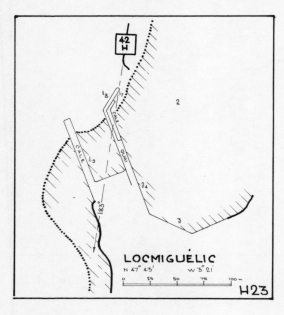

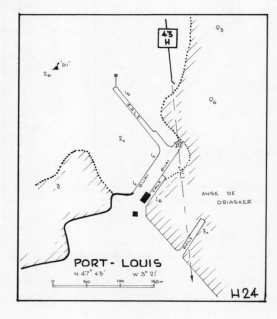

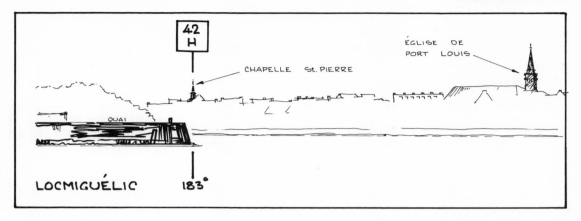

42H St Pierre chapel, Port Louis × the end of the quay keeps you clear of the sand banks. The south half of the quay is very convenient for drying against.

11—Port Louis

Formerly called Blavet, this fortified town renamed by Louis XIII is some hundreds of years older than Lorient, chart H24. To keep clear of the mud banks at the entrance use

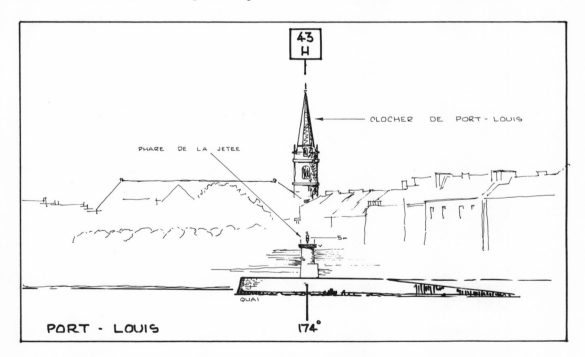

43H Port Louis church × the light at the end of the quay. The west side of the quay has been dredged to 1·0m and is used by a few trawlers, but the east side is seldom full. In the Anse de Driasker there are many moorings for local boats.

12—Locmalo

Seldom used by visiting yachts, this is worth more than passing interest since commercial traffic is absent, yet it is handy for Port Louis, chart H25. The best entrance is to start near Le Soulard *tourelle (isolée)* using view 28H, Passe de l'Ouest (p.104). Leave Le Soulard 30m to stb'd and come on a back mark

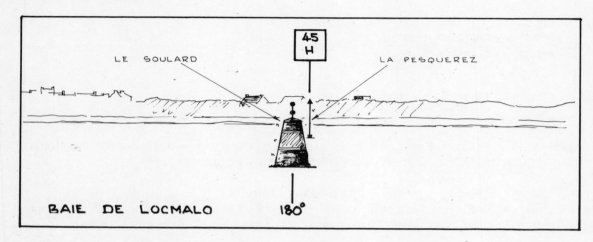

45H La Pesquerez *balise* × Le Soulard *tourelle (isolée)*. The mark for the stb'd turn north of Ile aux Souris is

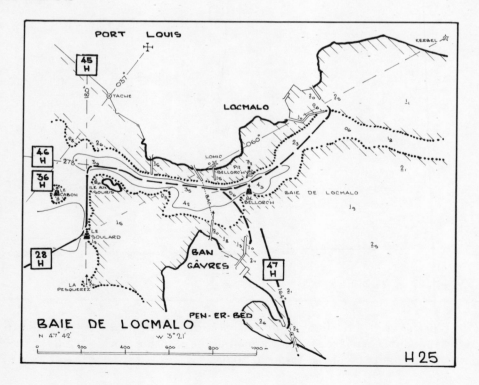

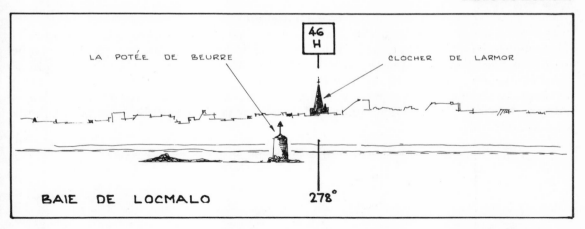

46H Larmor church × La Potée de Beurre. From now on you are in a scoured channel of over 3m and need only follow the recommended track on chart H25.

13—Ban-Gâvres

There is plenty of room for drying boats east or west of the quay, the best patch being between the two quays at the *1·8m* sounding. See chart H25.

14—Pen-er-Bed

This is the last harbour in Lorient and the slightly tongue-in-cheek mark,

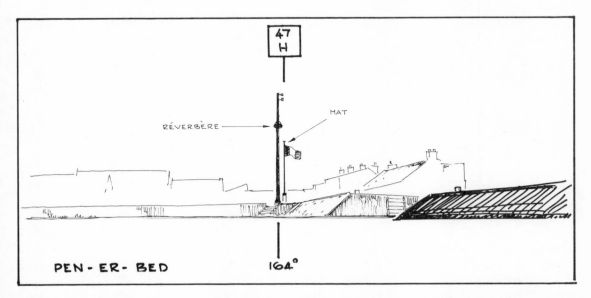

47H a flagstaff × a street lamp shows a channel through the mud. Once inside it is all lovely soft mud. The shops are at Ban-Gâvres, 500m distant.

15—Hennebont

Seven miles from Lorient up the Blavet River lies the old fortified medieval town of Hennebont, chart H26. The channel is well marked and is dredged to 3·5m for the first mile past Pointe de l'Espérance but the river is seldom less than 2m as far as the railway viaduct.

At Hennebont there are drying quays on the right bank and a pontoon for visitors on the left bank. Clearances beneath the three bridges on chart H26 are measured from HW springs and are therefore the absolute minimum. The railway viaduct must be passed through the central arch.

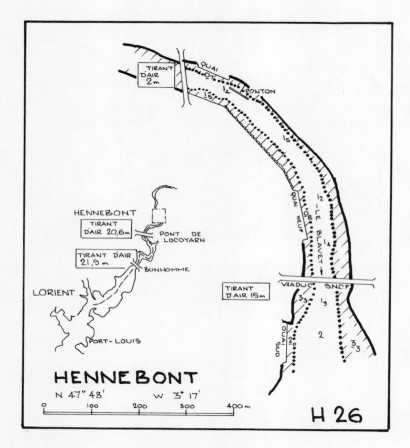

HENNEBONT

N 47° 48'   W 3° 17'

0   100   200   300   400 m

H 26

BASES DE VITESSE

The mystery of all those *amers* and *balises* we have been meeting since the Iles de Glénan—obviously of no navigational use—can now be explained. They are marks for measured distances, chart H27. The nearby naval base at Lorient must have had a field day during the last century, setting up the marks, though why they didn't make it easier for calculation—whole numbers of nautical miles—we shall never know. Tidal currents are here never more than a knot and run 280°/100° fortunately. The marks are still painted regularly, so you can settle finally that argument about your vessel's speed. I'm sorry I haven't pictured the pair of marks in Ile de Groix. The main axis is

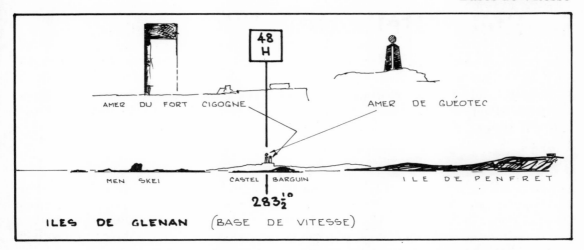

AMER DU FORT CIGOGNE

AMER DE GUÉOTEC

48H

MEN SKEI

CASTEL BARGUIN

ILE DE PENFRET

283½°

ILES DE GLÉNAN (BASE DE VITESSE)

48H the *amer* of Fort Cigogne × Guéotec *amer*. Both these are in Iles de Glénan and are shown on chart G26 (p.71). Breast marks are

4H (p.83) the *balise* of Raguénès × the *amer* on Ile Verte,

7H (p.88) Riec church, *amer* of Riec, *amer* of Kerfany and *amer* of Kerhermain all in line, and

10H (p.91) *Amer* of Pencleu × the two lighthouses of Doëlan.

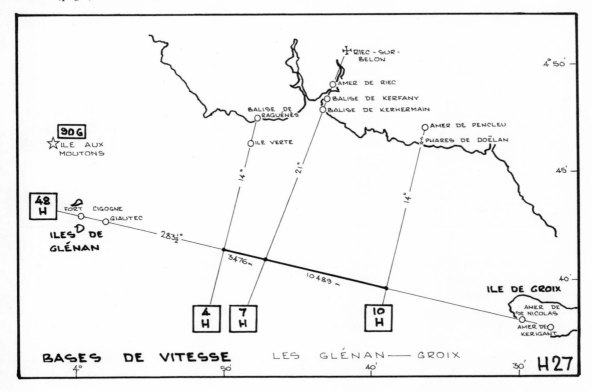

BASES DE VITESSE   LES GLÉNAN — GROIX   H27

I Étel to Belle Ile

Here is the end of Lower Brittany where the rocky cliffs give way to sandy estuaries, low-lying islands and marshes and, if it's any help to you, it was in Quiberon Bay that Admiral Hawke defeated de Conflans thus scotching any fears of a French invasion of England.

ÉTEL

Here is one of those indecisive harbours with a constantly moving bar of varying depth, chart I1. You will notice that I show the bar either drying 5·0m or with half a metre of water and they tell stories in Étel like the one about the trawler which came in for shelter one day and had to wait seven weeks for enough water to get out again. I've been in three times without mishap, so, with prayer book in one hand and tide tables in the other, try

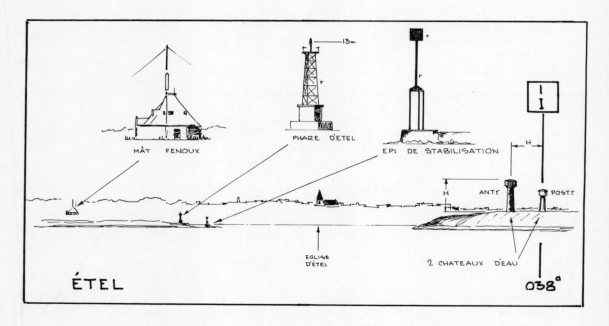

MÂT FENOUX PHARE D'ETEL EPI DE STABILISATION H ANTE POSTE H 2 CHATEAUX D'EAU EGLISE D'ETEL 13m

ÉTEL 038°

I2 two water towers open as shown. The best time is about 1–2 hours before high water when the flood, bearing in mind it has to fill 10 square miles of estuary, will have eased off. A cable before reaching the port *balise* on the *épi de stabilisation* you will be in the scoured channel, so keep about 100m from this training wall and then no more than a cable from the right bank of the river. Once you are abreast of the first water tower there is ample depth, 6–8m.

Chart I2 shows the harbour and there is usually plenty of room in the river on the west-facing quays. Or you might try the *port de plaisance* north of the harbour office. Probably on account of the fearsome entrance, fewer than a dozen fishing boats live here.

The harbour authorities would be offended should I not mention their Fenoux signal mast just north of the lighthouse. I have never seen it working nor met anyone who has, but then, as a French yachtsman was heard to explain, neither have I ever seen a rabbit playing a *biniou*. I am assured though that if you telephone (97) 52-35-59, during daytime, not earlier than half-tide, at one hour's minimum notice, not forgetting to hoist your ensign to the masthead on approach, all will be well. The signals are fairly simple:

A   The arrow on the mast will oscillate from right to left about ten times to show that you have been seen.

B   If you are correctly placed the arrow will point upwards.

C   If you are not, the arrow will point to the side to which you must steer.

D   If the arrow is horizontal, surmounted by a ball, entrance is forbidden.

E   A red flag means there is not enough water.

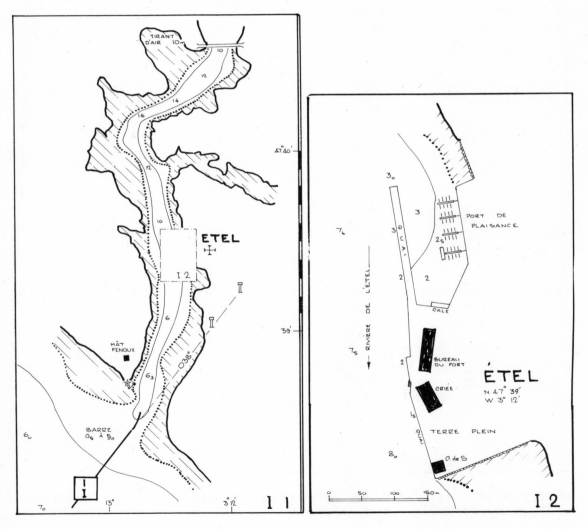

PORTIVY

To calm your shattered nerves on coming out of Étel, try this snug little drying harbour on the west side of the Quiberon peninsula. On the way south from Étel to clear all the shoals inside Les Pierres Noires use

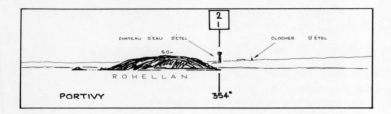

2I Étel high water tower just to the right of Rohelan (5·0m high). This takes you on to chart I3 and the first entrance mark is

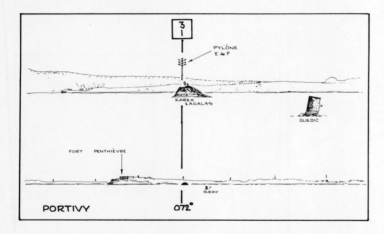

3I an electricity pylon × Karek Lagalas (*8·5m*). There are a row of these pylons about a km apart on the route serving Quiberon, but only one fits the bearing shown. When just before Guedic port hand buoy, find

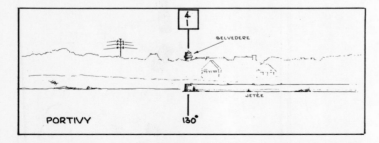

4I the tower of an old mill × the end of the jetty. The harbour is on chart I4 where there is usually plenty of drying room at the south end.

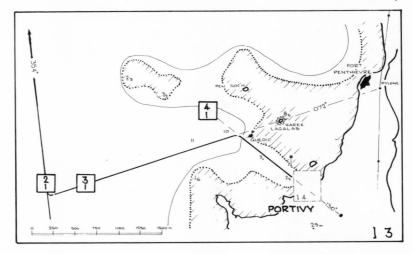

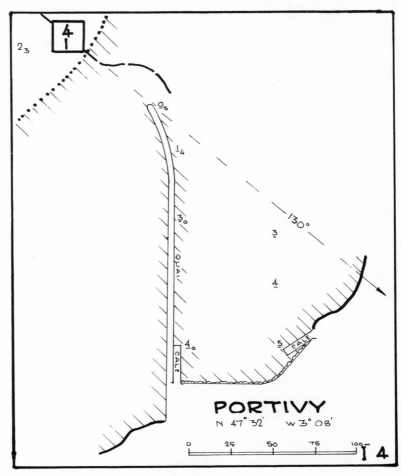

PORTIVY

N 47° 32'   W 3° 08'

PORT-MARIA

This is the harbour of the town of Quiberon, also called Loc Maria but of course nowadays together with Port Haliguen, forms one unit called Quiberon. The harbour is shown on chart I5 and just west of it stands a prominent landmark, the Château Beg-er-Lann pictured on the only mark necessary,

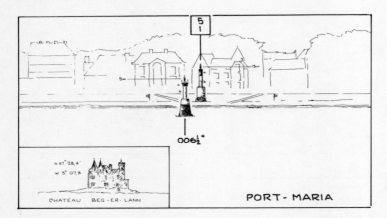

5I the two lights on the beach in line. The east mole is reserved for the Belle Ile ferry: the south breakwater is mostly foul and the adjacent area devoted to fishing boat moorings but a drying berth can sometimes be found on the north side of the Vieux Môle.

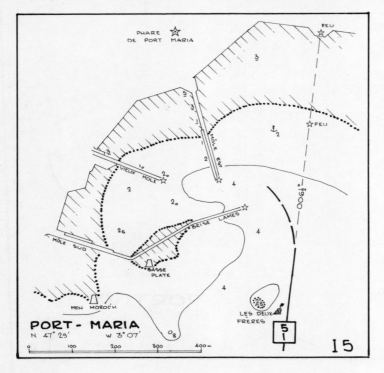

There are several channels into Quiberon bay, those that require marks being shown on chart I6. The Chenal de Béniguet is described later and is on chart I12 (p.137):

1—Passage de la Teignouse
2—Passage de la Basse Nouvelle
3—Chenal des Trois Pierres
4—Chenal d'Er-Toul-Bras

The channels are described in the sense west to east.

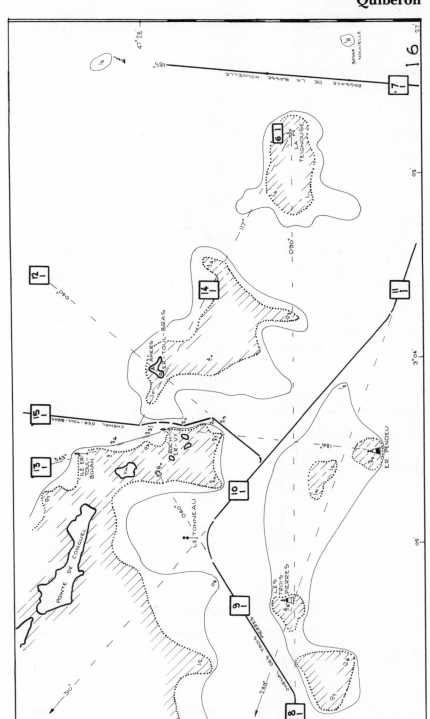

1—Passage de la Teignouse (16·0m)

The entrance starts a cable south of the Goué Vas Sud lit buoy where you are in the centre of the white sector of the Teignouse light. No marks can be given, but in any case the channel is seldom less than half a mile wide.

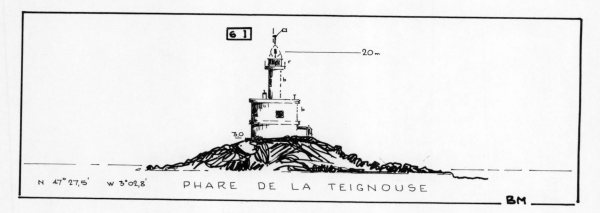

N 47° 27,5′   W 3° 02,8′   PHARE DE LA TEIGNOUSE   BM

6I A view of the light which must be kept bearing 036°. When a cable south of the Goué Vas Est lit buoy steer 068° to leave the Basse Nouvelle lit buoy to port and the NE Teignouse lit buoy to stb'd. The whole channel is only two miles long from first to last buoys.

2—Passage de la Basse Nouvelle (8·4m)

To save time when sailing north from the Passage de la Teignouse, use the short cut, a back mark which clears between the lighthouse and Basse Nouvelle (1·3m) Chart I6 (p.123)

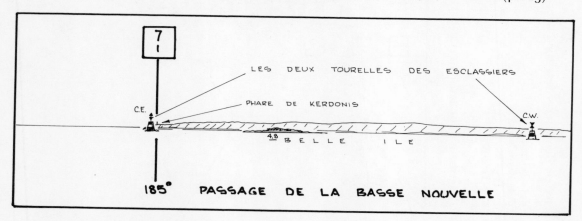

185°   PASSAGE DE LA BASSE NOUVELLE

7I Kerdonis light, in Belle Ile ✕ the left hand of the two Esclassiers *tourelles*.

3—Chenal des Trois Pierres (2·5m)

This starts off 3 cables south of Le Four *tourelle* and the lead-in mark is

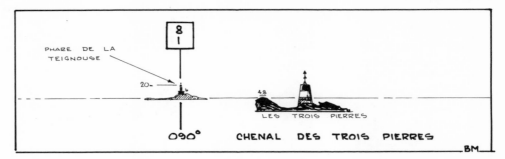

8I the Teignouse light to the left of Les Trois Pierres *tourelle* (CN) Chart I6 (p.123). When 3 cables off this *tourelle*, steer to port on

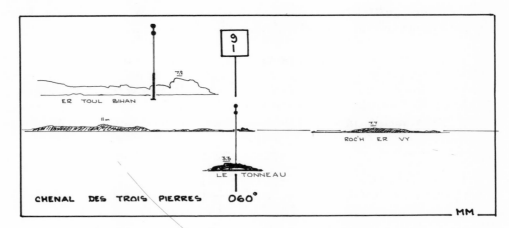

9I the south head of Er Toul Bihan (*7·2m*) × Le Tonneau *balise (isolée)*. When a cable from the *balise* make a handrail south and take a back mark

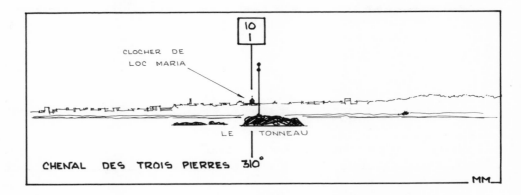

10I Loc Maria church by the same *balise*, Le Tonneau. A mile down this transit, take the final exit back mark

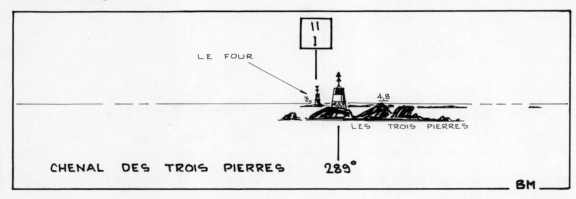

CHENAL DES TROIS PIERRES 289°

11I Le Four *tourelle* (CS) × Les Trois Pierres *tourelle* (CN). This channel holds no terrors since the important first and last marks use man-made objects.

4—Chenal d'Er-Toul-Bras (2·0m)

This is a useful short cut between Quiberon and Port Haliguen and it is best taken at low water because then not only will there be no swell, but the sides of the channel will be more clearly marked. It starts off from the Chenal des Trois Pierres 4 cables north of Er Pendeu *tourelle* (CS) Chart 16 (p.123). Man-made objects are used throughout and the first mark is

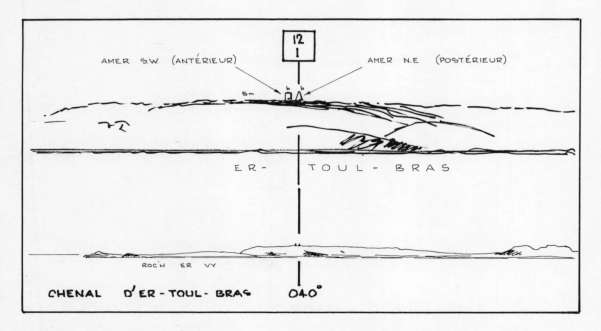

CHENAL D'ER-TOUL-BRAS 040°

12I the two white *amers* on Er-Toul-Bras open exactly as shown. Stand by for a smart port turn on to

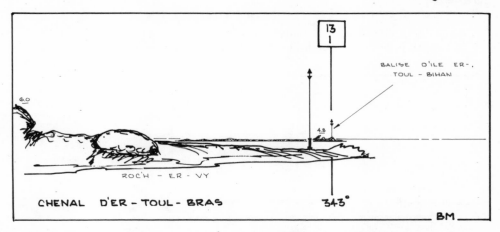

13I the Er-Toul-Bihan *balise* × Roc'h-er-Vy *balise* (both CE). If possible keep them open as shown. Make a handrail east-about from the nearer *balise* allowing 25m off until a breast mark comes up,

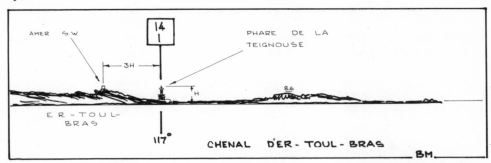

14I the Teignouse lighthouse open to the right of the SW *amer* on Er-Toul-Bras. This is the cue to take the exit back mark.

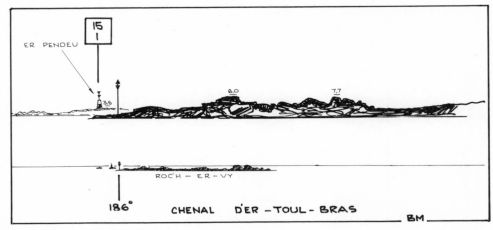

15I Er Pendeu *tourelle* to the left of Roc'h-er-Vy *balise*.

PORT HALIGUEN

Here is a safe marina with easy access in a sheltered bay, chart I7. The only entrance that needs a mark is from the north and to keep you clear of shore dangers take

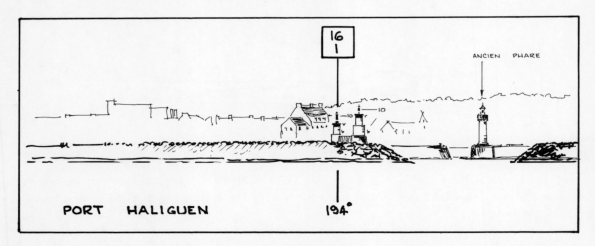

PORT HALIGUEN   194°

16I the two east lighthouses in line. There is nothing that needs explanation inside; there is everything for a yachtsman, with 600 places including 100 for visitors.

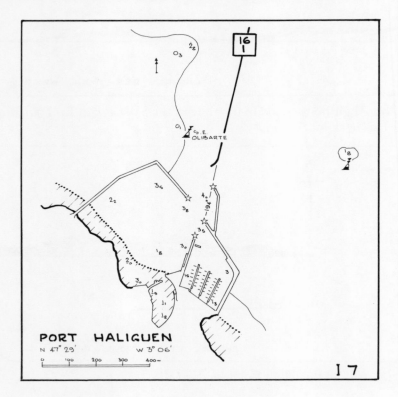

PORT HALIGUEN

N 47° 29'   W 3° 06'

0   100   200   300   400 ~

I 7

ST PIERRE (PORT D'ORANGE)

A mere two miles north of Port Haliguen is this unassuming little drying harbour, chart I8. The deepest channel is

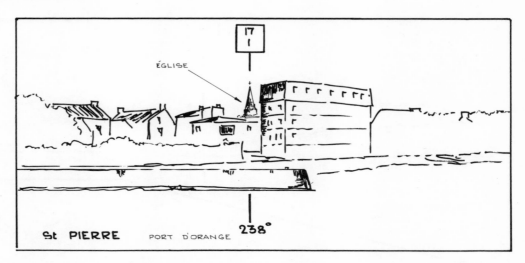

17I the church just peeping to the left of a large block of flats.

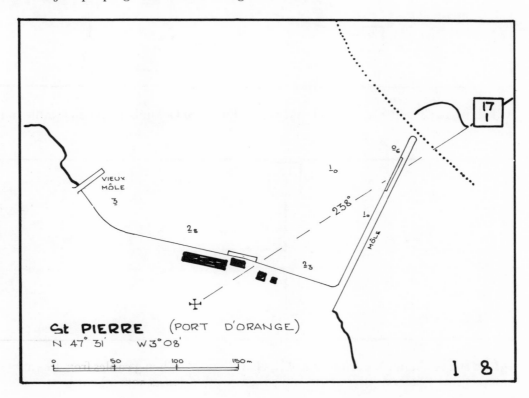

LE PO

Chart I9 shows this oyster river, the one-time port for Carnac. Approaching from the south, take

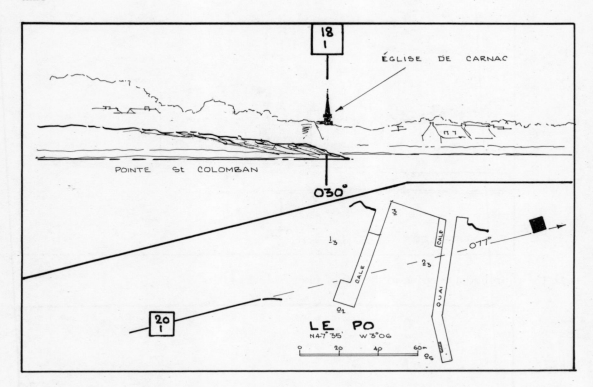

18I Carnac church × the right hand side of Pointe St Colomban. When 3 cables off turn to port on

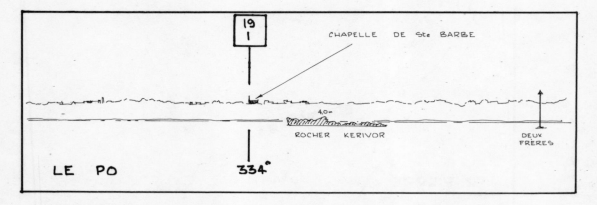

19I St Barbe chapel × the left side of Rocher Kerivor. When 3 cables from this above-water group of rocks, steer north so as to leave the two stb'd *balises* 50m off until

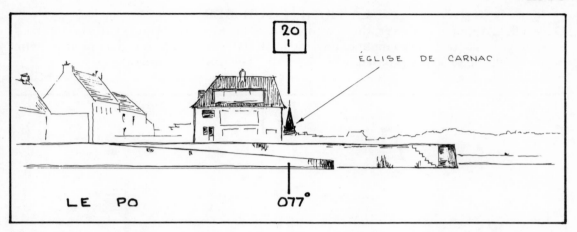

20I Carnac church × the right side of a large house on the quay. The harbour plan (on view 18I) shows everything. The east quay can be used both sides. It is only a 1½ km walk to Carnac.

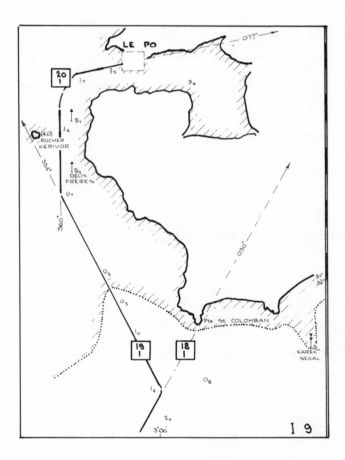

LA TRINITÉ-SUR-MER

Once a flourishing oyster river, this harbour is now the most important centre on this coast for sailing. It is accessible by night or day and at all states of the tide and gives perfect shelter for the thousand or so boats based here, chart I10. The daytime marks are

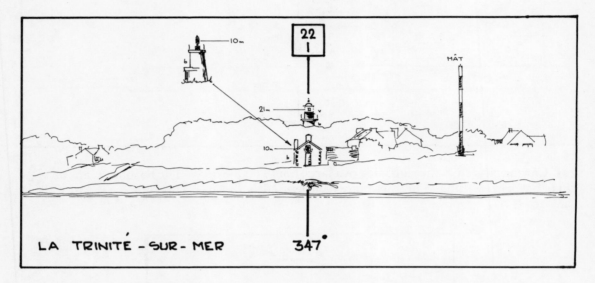

22I the two lighthouses in line. The front light is sectored. When 3 cables off the light, take a stern mark,

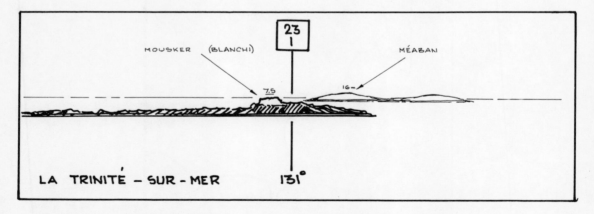

23I Méaban to the right of the white rock Mousker. The final mark

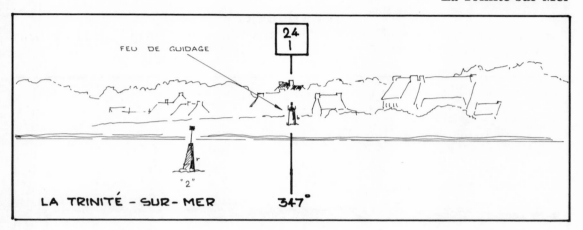

24I is provided by a sectored light at 347° and from here on the channel is buoyed (chart I11). The first pontoon past the quay (opposite the 3·1m sounding) is for visitors. The Kerisper bridge has a clearance of 18m minimum, above which are very many moorings in the river.

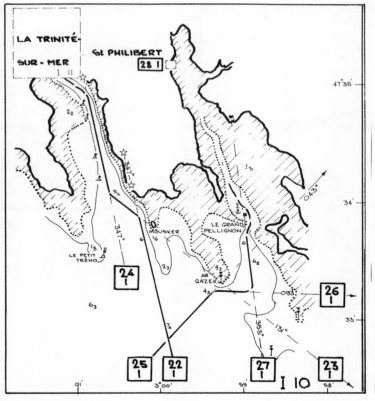

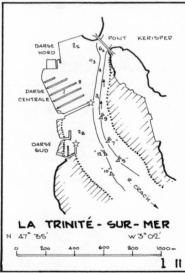

133

ST PHILIBERT

A complete contrast to its neighbour, this village is shown on chart I 10 (p.133). The entrance starts from the La Trinité marks,

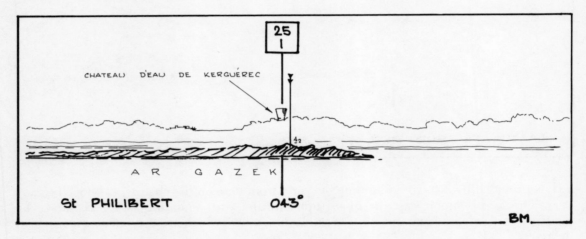

25I Kerguérec water tower × Ar Gazek *balise* (CS). A cable from the *balise* change to

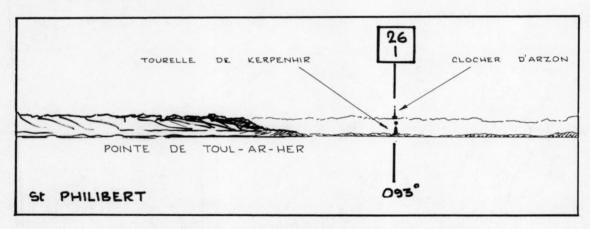

26I Arzon church × Kerpenhir *tourelle*. Make a sharp port turn when

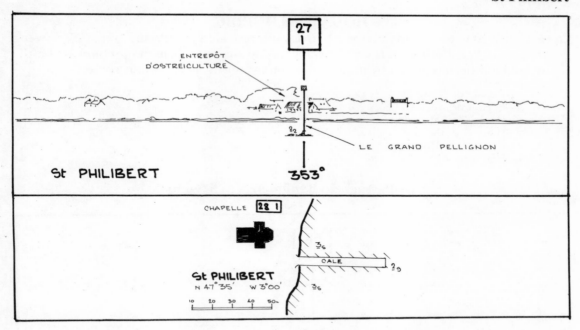

27I the buildings of an oyster farm × Le Grand Pellignon *balise*. Leave this *balise* 20m to port and carry on up the channel which is marked by withies. You will see that there is 2m about here, a most convenient place at which to anchor. A mile up the river, you come to the hamlet of St Philibert,

28I this shows the tiny chapel (1785) built alongside the slip which I shared only with a flock of sandpipers.

HOUAT and HOËDIC

Once connected to the mainland, these twin islands provide a fascinating miniature cruising ground, chart I12. Both islands are the same in that their old disused harbours are on the south and have been replaced by modern ones on the north. There are six routes:

  1—Passage du Béniguet
  2—Passage des Soeurs
  3—Houat from the north
  4—Houat from the west
  5—Hoëdic from Houat
  6—Hoëdic, new harbour to old

1—Passage du Béniguet, N to S (20m)

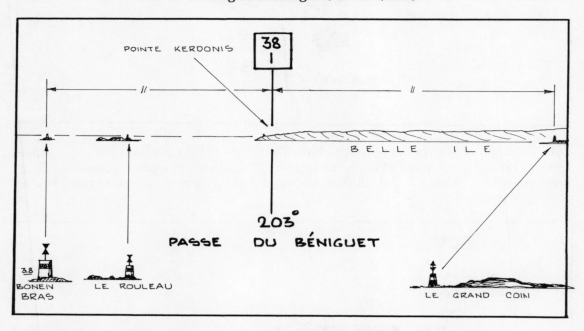

38I Pointe de Kerdonis, Belle Ile midway between the two *tourelles* of Bonen Bras and Le Grand Coin. Having passed this gateway, there are no dangers on the south, but leave le Rouleau a couple of cables to port.

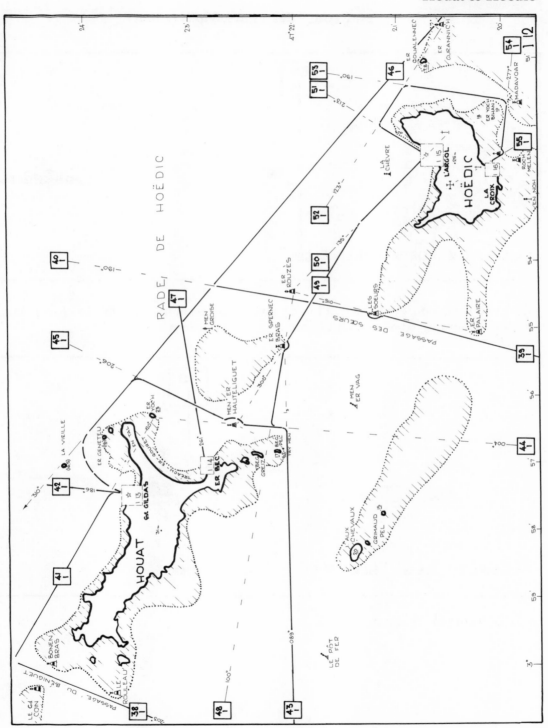

2—Passage des Sœurs, S to N (4.6m)

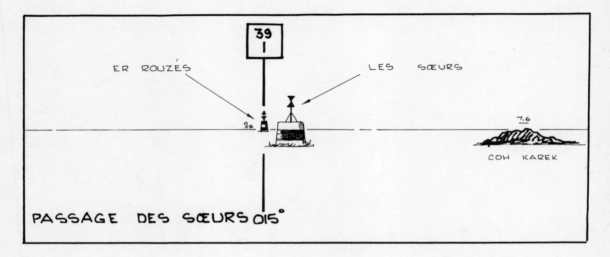

39I Er Rouzès *tourelle* to the left of Les Sœurs. On no account must they be closed. Make a handrail 100m west-about round Les Sœurs and take a stern mark

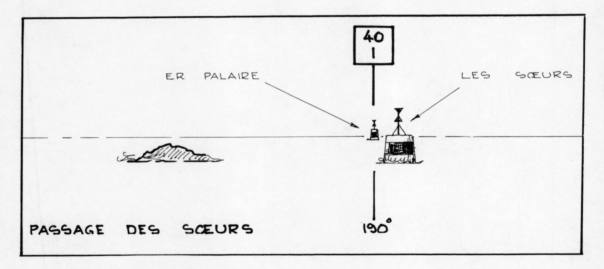

40I Er Palaire by Les Sœurs *tourelle*.

3—Houat from the N (3·4m)

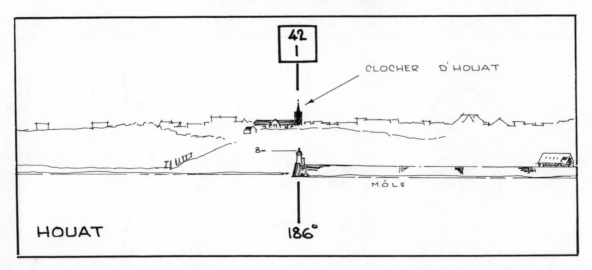

CLOCHER D'HOUAT

42
I

8m

MÔLE

HOUAT

186°

42I The church on Houat by the lighthouse at the end of the quay. This is used at night in the white sector of the light and clears to the west of La Vieille. If you have come via the Passage du Béniguet, bear away using

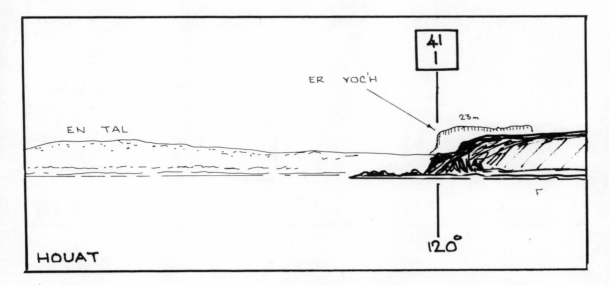

41
I

ER YOC'H

EN TAL

23m

F

HOUAT

120°

41I the left of Er Yoc'h just seen by the cliff next to the sandy spit of land En Tal. This joins view 42I to take you on to chart I13 (p.140). The harbour, correctly called Port St Gildas, is usually crowded with fishing boats and as the south quay is reserved for the Quiberon ferries, it's a good plan to anchor outside in 6m where shown.

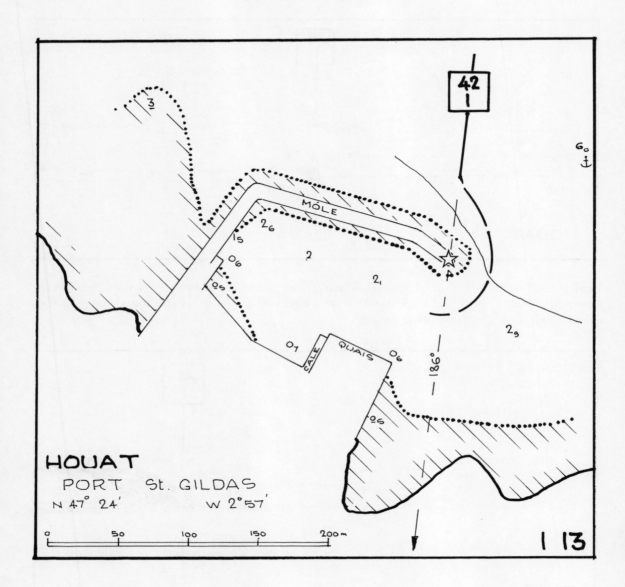

HOUAT

PORT St. GILDAS

N 47° 24'   W 2°57'

4—Houat from the W (2·0m)

Start just north of Le Pôt de Fer buoy (*isolée*),

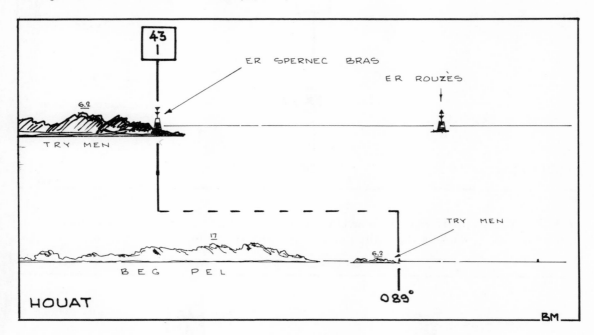

43I Er Spernec Bras *tourelle* just seen at the right of Try Men. This is the most southerly outlier of three large high rocks (*17–20m*) off the south end of Houat. Leave Try Men 50m to port and when 2 cables past take a right-angled port turn

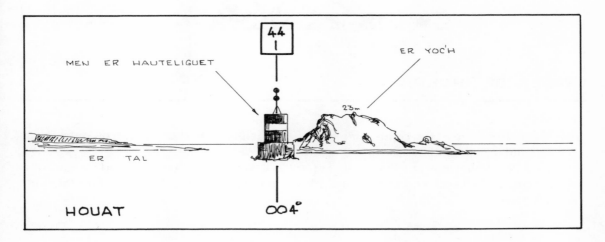

44I a giant of a rock Er Yoc'h seen to the right of Men er Hauteliguet (*isolée*). Leave this *tourelle* 50m to port and take a back mark,

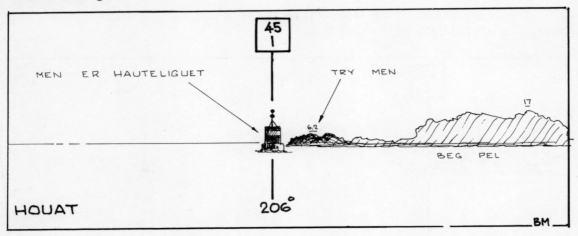

45I Try Men to the right of Men er Hauteliguet. When past Er Yoc'h you can look for an important safety mark for the entire north-east side of the archipelago,

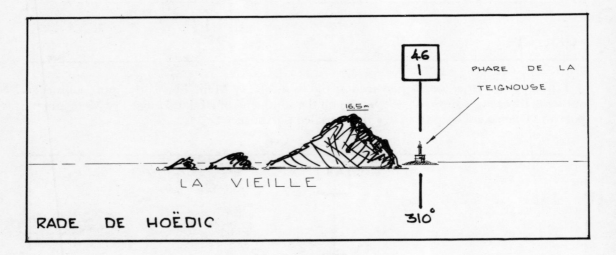

46I Teignouse light × the right-hand side of La Vieille. This mark leads you outside Er Geneteu and from here it is clear into the harbour.

To find the old harbour, Er Bec, chart I14, retrace your steps to view 45I and the harbour can be seen at the south end of that magnificent mile-long beach, Tréach-er-Gouret. The harbour mark is

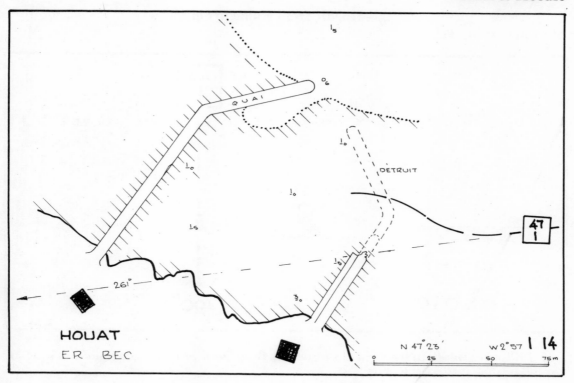

HOUAT

ER BEC

N 47°23'   W 2°57   **1 14**

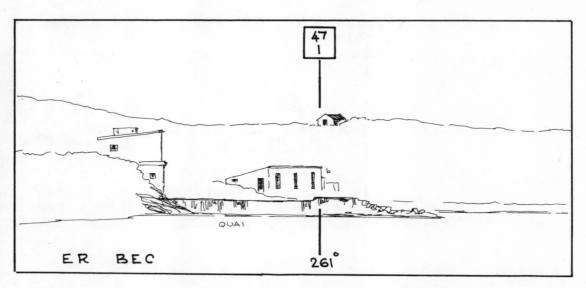

ER BEC

47I a small stone hut × the right side of a disused store. This harbour was destroyed in the 'fifties but still provides a solitary berth for a night or two. There are two shops near the church in Houat. Water and fuel are scarce.

5—Hoëdic from Houat (6·0m)

Start off near Beg Pel by

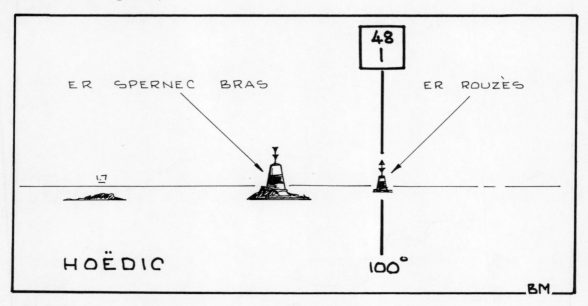

48I Er Rouzès *tourelle* to the right of Er Spernec Bras *tourelle*. Make a 50m handrail south of the latter, then take a back mark,

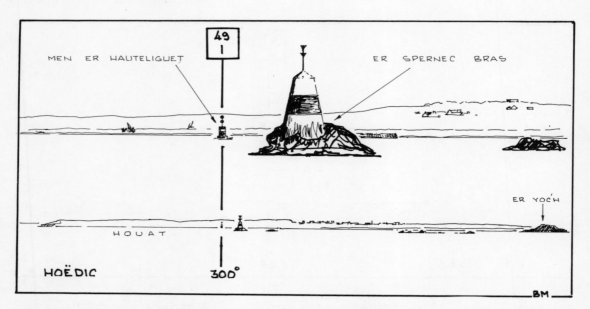

49I Men er Hauteliguet × the left of Er Spernec Bras. The final mark for the harbour, Port de l'Argol, is

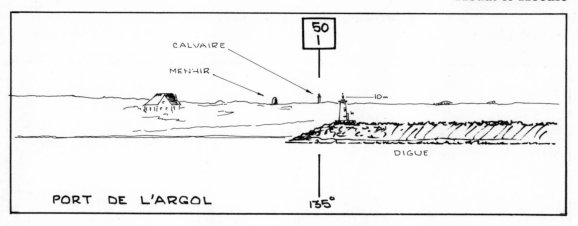

PORT DE L'ARGOL

50I a calvary ✕ the harbour lighthouse. This cramped harbour is on chart I15, the accessible part of the quay being reserved for the Quiberon ferries. Hoëdic has even fewer facilities than Houat.

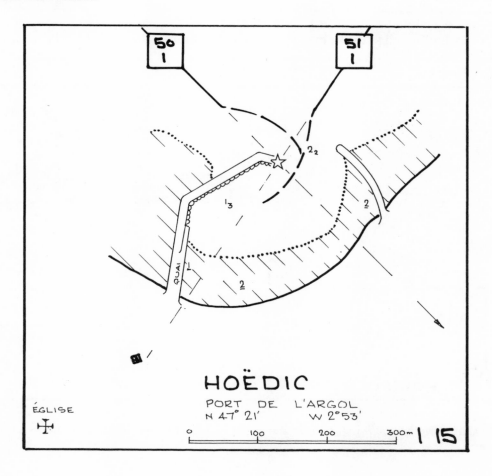

HOËDIC
PORT DE L'ARGOL
N 47° 21'   W 2° 53'

6—Hoëdic, new harbour to old (0·5m)

We will start off from Port de l'Argol with a short mark to clear the rocks outside the harbour,

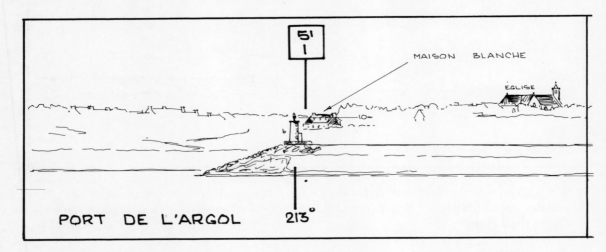

51I a white house well to the right of the harbour lighthouse. When clear of the north point, look for

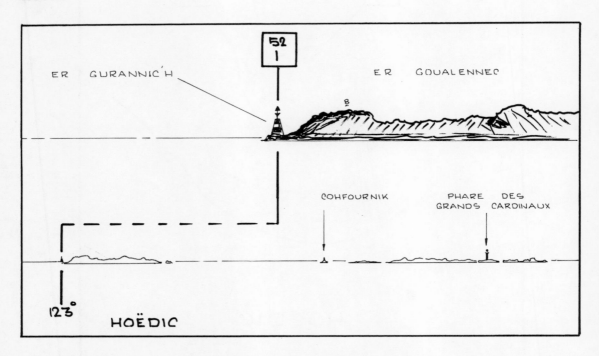

52I Er Gurannic'h *tourelle* just seen to the left of Er Goualennec. To take you down the east side use

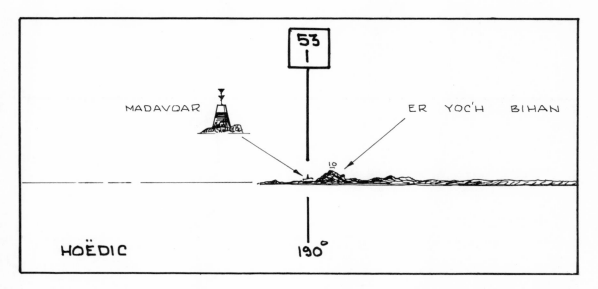

53I Madavoar *tourelle* × Er Yoc'h Bihan (*10·0m*). Leave this rock 50m to stb'd and a cable before Madavoar take

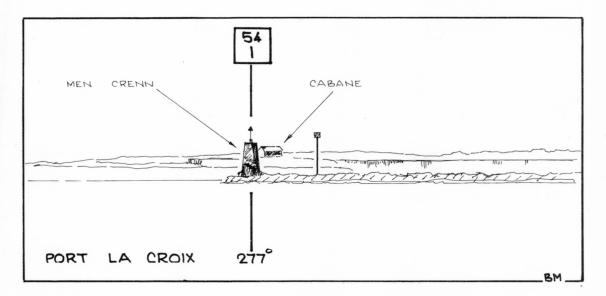

54I an old stone hut exactly as shown to the right of Men Crenn *tourelle*. This turn is in the shallowest and narrowest part of the channel but as you approach Men Crenn it gets deeper. Dodge 50m south of Men Crenn and head for the harbour on

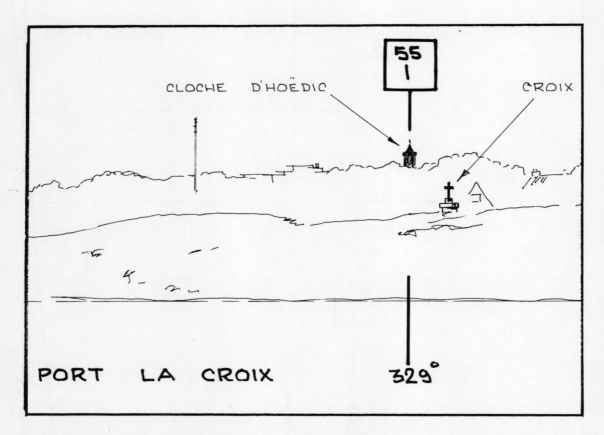

CLOCHE D'HOËDIC

CROIX

55
1

PORT LA CROIX

329°

55I Hoëdic church to the left of a cross on the beach. Chart I16 shows the rather lonely harbour of Port la Croix and it is very likely you will be the only boat occupying it. You can choose your berth.

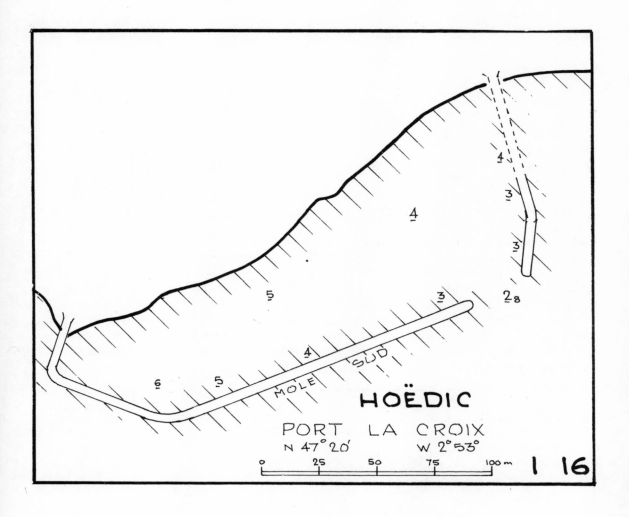

HOËDIC

PORT LA CROIX
N 47° 20'   W 2° 53°

| 0 | 25 | 50 | 75 | 100 m |

1 16

BELLE ILE

Raided by the Saracens, the Saxons, Normans, Spaniards and Dutch it was twice occupied by the British who finally swapped it for Nova Scotia. With a bit of luck you might discover that mythical undersea passage connecting it to the mainland.

Le Palais

The capital is Le Palais on chart I17 and a somewhat irrelevant mark is

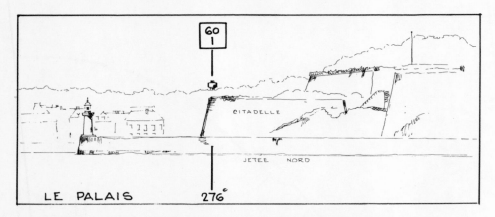

6oI a water tower × Fouquet's citadel which dates from 1650.

The harbour naturally becomes crowded but with perseverance you can nearly always find a berth. The ferries from Quiberon belt in and out of the harbour frequently, using the Quai Macé. They spend the night stern to the Môle Bourdelles. There are buoys opposite the Quai Bonnelle and the Môle Bourdelles. The citadel side of the *arriére port* usually has plenty of drying berths free along the Quai Trochu. Fishing boats occupy the rest but if you want perfect peace, lock through into the wet basin. The lock is open in daytime only, one hour before to one hour after high water; night time and Sundays on demand. Le Palais has all the facilities of a fishing port of 3000 inhabitants.

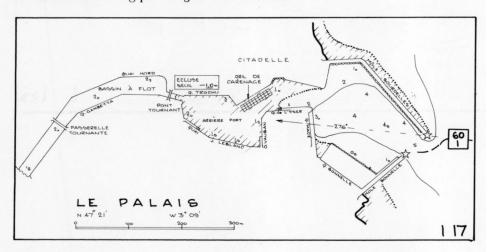

Sauzon

4 miles to the north is this most attractive little drying harbour, chart 118. Recently breakwaters have been built giving deep water moorings at the entrance. The mark is

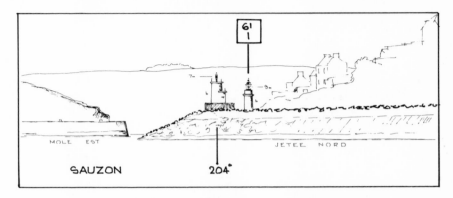

61I the old lighthouse × the new north jetty light. A few fishing boats use the west mole, but the drying quays further up on the west side are often free. A snug berth is inside the east mole but you will have to wait for low water to walk across to the shops.

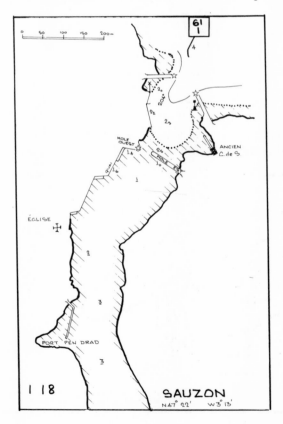

Stêr Ouen

Here is a fascinating little creek among the rocks just to the south of Pointe des Poulains, chart I19. The entrance is deep and with boldness can be taken in most weather.

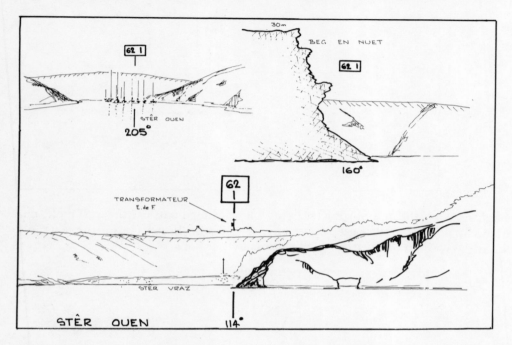

62I A pole transformer exactly as shown touching a point of land. there is a smaller pole on the beach almost on the same transit. The same sketch shows Beg en Nuet which will help to locate your position before entering. There are no marks for the abrupt stb'd turn, and the whole anchorage, though narrow, is 300m long. There are no shops within a thousand miles!

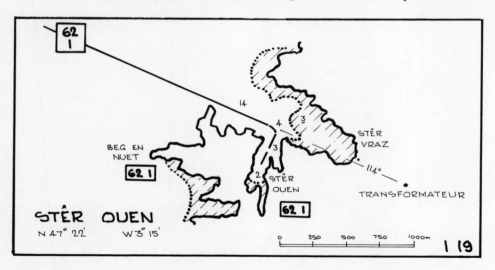

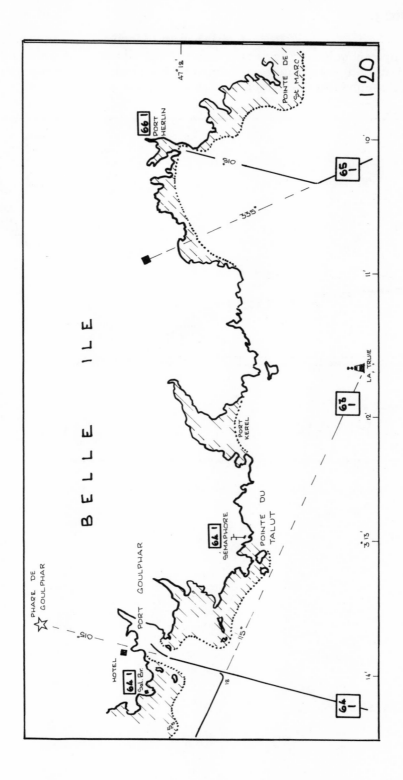

Ports Goulphar and Herlin

There are umpteen night stop anchorages more or less all round the coast of Belle Ile but on the south coast there are a couple worth mentioning specially. They are both on chart I20 (p.153) and if coming from the west a good safety mark is

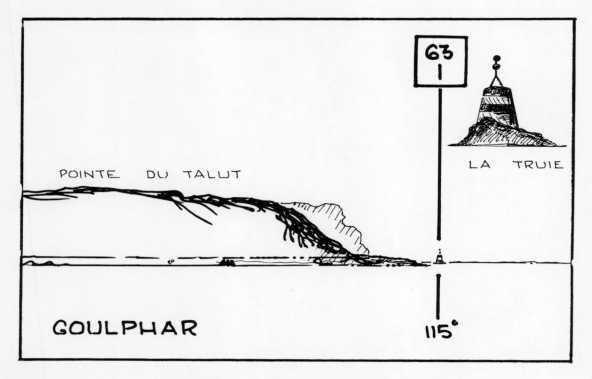

63I La Truie seen open of Pointe du Talut. The marks for Goulphar are

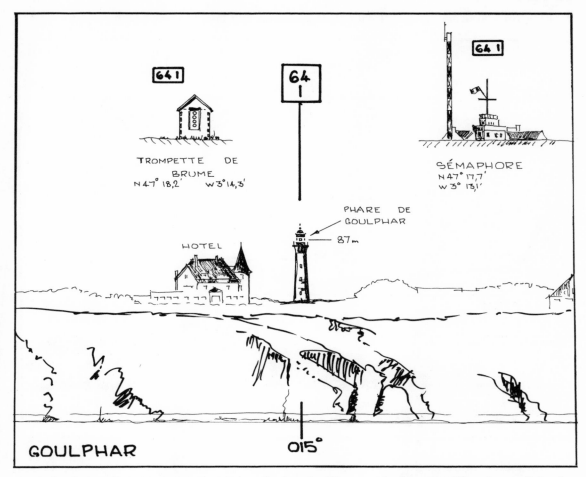

64I Goulphar lighthouse to the right of a hotel with a conical tower. The views of the fog signal and the semaphore might help since the cliffs are high and featureless.

French Pilot 3

Port Herlin is another creek but with a sandy beach, the safe approach being

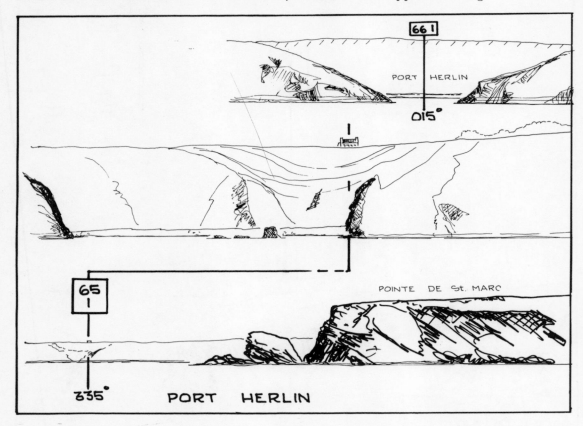

65I an isolated house × the right hand side of a beach, for which I can't give you any better mark than

66I (on the same sketch as 65I) the gap in the rocks at 015°.

How fitting that we should end with a lonely unimportant creek similar to the one we started with way back on the Pointe du Raz. I have described entries to over 70 places and I think you will agree that the charm of the 150 miles of coast has been above all else the contrast in harbours from those poky creeks to the vast commercial harbours, from the wide estuaries to those sheltered rivers, never forgetting the half dozen colourful islands.

Index

Harbours and anchorages only are indexed